—— YOUR ——
LEADERSHIP
EDGE

MASTER MANAGMENT SKILLS FOR TODAY'S WORKFORCE

RAVINDER TULSIANI

Published by CreateSpace Independent Publishing Platform, North Charleston, SC.

For additional copies/bulk purchases of this book visit: www.yourleadershipedge.ca

ISBN-13: 978-1500148232
ISBN-10: 1500148237
LCCN: 2014922382
BISAC: Business & Economics / Leadership

Library of Congress Cataloging-in-Publication Data
Tulsiani, Ravinder
    Your Leadership Edge : Mastering Management Skills For Today's Workforce / by Ravinder Tulsiani – 1st ed.
    ISBN-13: 978-1-5001-4823-2

Printed in the United States of America

ACKNOWLEDGEMENTS

After years of industry experience and months of in-depth research, I have merged all of my expertise and industry knowledge into this book. This book would not have been possible had it not been for the experience I gained through my own work experience. I'd like to acknowledge with a heartfelt thank you all of those who came before me – from mentors, industry experts, educators, colleagues, and, more recently, media outlets that acknowledged that my information and experience had value and gave me a platform with which to share my insights. Most importantly, I'd like to thank my family and my dear friends. Without you, I would not be the man I am today.

PREFACE

Your Leadership Edge was born in response to an observation of a disturbing trend within the business community – a rapid decline in overall employee performance. Noticing this trend, I started to emphasize to management the importance of a high level of engagement to the department efficiency and to the company's bottom-line.

This led me to the belief that a positive well-trained leader can create an optimal work environment and drive company growth exponentially, while an ill-equipped leader will simply drive good employees away and potentially amplify costs of ongoing recruitment and training.

Your Leadership EDGE is a training program designed to help you develop the core competencies needed to become an exceptional leader, enabling you to engage and develop your employees, so that you can drive massive growth to your organization.

It is my hope that by using the step-by-step program outlined in each of the chapters in this book, you will not only become more aware of the core leadership competencies; you will acquire the necessary leadership skills foundation that will enable you to develop and support a highly engaged and productive workforce.

CONTENTS

CHAPTER I

HOW THIS BOOK WILL HELP YOU

AS A LEADER, you may be faced with many hard questions. A successful leader knows how to interpret those questions and transform them into solutions.

This book will serve as your leadership mentor and will enable you to identify and maximize your core leadership qualities. Doing so will support you in developing a highly engaged and productive staff.

Team members rely on their leaders to guide them through their daily tasks. An effective leader will not only guide staff, but will stimulate them to reach their full potential. Identifying exactly what kind of leader you are is the first task you must complete to meet the challenges of today's workforce.

As we continue, we will begin discussing and dissecting leadership styles and determine what it takes to develop your style into proven strategies for success. We will look at the qualities of a good leader and determine whether or not those are qualities you possess and/or help you to develop those qualities and teach you how to use that skill set to take control of a team and effectively use their strengths and abilities

9

to their maximum potential – thus, garnering a much more productive, happy, self-confident workforce that meets and/or beats their goals and is motivated to strive for success and expand their scope to meet the growing needs of your company.

We will help you to determine your competency gaps and will create a plan of action to eliminate that separation and give you the tools you need to continue to thrive in your demanding position. Like all savvy professionals, a leader is never done developing. A strong effective leader continues to grow and adapt to meet the needs of clients and staff. They will not rest on their laurels waiting for the market to revert back to their comfort levels, but will seek out more information and begin to utilize more effective strategies and will develop their own skills in order to provide credible leadership to those whom depend on them for guidance. These ever-changing skills will complement the overall growth of their team and will enhance the abilities of the team as a whole.

Once you've mastered the necessary skills, they will enable you to produce results and increase the potential of your team members. The team is anxiously waiting for you to lead them using your perfected leadership skill set.

Core competencies are crucial for anyone in a leadership/ management position. Knowing what these competencies are is the first step, but understanding and putting those competencies to use is what sets you apart from other leaders. Possessing these competencies places you well ahead of your competition and solidifies you into a league of your own by increasing your credibility, your trustworthiness, and increasing your self-confidence allowing your team to benefit from your wealth of knowledge.

The natural question to ask here is 'What are core competencies?' The answer is not as complex as one might think. Here, we will provide an overview of those competencies and you may be surprised by some of them. You may even believe you have them. That's a start. In the next few chapters, we will expand on those competencies and put them to use for you.

1 **Conflict Resolution** - Understanding where conflict stems from is a major component to being able to resolve it before it escalates. Having this ability is paramount for a leader. Know that conflict arises from differences. These differences can be large or small. There is no hard and fast rule. In the workplace, for our purposes, conflict can wreak havoc on morale. How you handle that conflict is in direct correlation to how you'll be perceived as a leader. People disagree. That's normal. However, their reactions to that are rooted in their values, perceptions, motivations, and ideas. An effective leader will understand that and will without choosing sides nurture and support their team members while examining what caused the conflict initially and make an objective decision and create a plan to circumvent any further rife. Doing so may result in intact deals, larger profits, job security, and stronger team morale.

2 **Time Management** - Utilizing great time management strategies allows you time to focus on pertinent and urgent tasks. That goes without saying. However, to employ good time management skills you must be able to clearly define them. Avoiding crisis to begin with by completing tasks as required and free of error will nullify any prospect of having to revisit that task again. Another aspect to avoid is procrastination. There's no room for it in business. As the saying goes 'time is money' and you nor your employer are in the business of throwing away money. To increase revenues, you must remain productive and charge head first into your assigned duties. Regardless of how big or small the task is, move ahead with it by implementing a plan to conquer it in its entirety. Another key to ineffective time management is having unrealistic expectations. You are only at work for so many hours and creating a mental checklist with a plethora of tasks assigned to it is setting yourself up for

failure. Allow time for interruption and set up a realistic time frame to complete that checklist with quality work and not a rushed delivery thus creating unnecessary stress for yourself and your team. Lastly, understand and make sure your team fully understands what their roles are and how and when to carry out the duties associated with those roles. As a cohesive team, you will be more efficient and confident doing jobs that you are trained to do and you are confident you'll be able to complete.

3   **Delegate Successfully** - This management skill benefits everyone in the workplace. Know your team and understand what they as individuals and a team are capable of. Be logical in your thinking when assigning tasks. Do not deviate from their scope of knowledge or skills. Giving employees an impossible task that they have no knowledge of will not only frustrate them, but will frustrate you and will demotivate them to want to help. Successful delegation frees up time for yourself and your team as a whole. Prior to assigning a task, ensure that you understand how to do the task yourself so that you may better explain the expectations to the person you are assigning and so that you won't have to micromanage them. Assigning a task and then hovering over the employee severs their confidence and destroys any semblance of trust they may have had in you as their leader. As the leader, it is your job to monitor without hovering and to review the task once it's completed. Your responsibility doesn't end with that review, you must then provide relevant feedback in a timely fashion. Doing this will relegate them to want to continue to work harder and will keep them motivated to acquire more skills.

3   **Communication** – Actively listening to your employees encourages their expression of ideas and opinions. A strong leader is not intimidated by the input their employees may have. They will welcome it and will lead better for having

done so. Learning to communicate via the proper channels is another important facet to good communication in the workplace. Know when it is appropriate to send and/or receive messages via email or whether or not a conversation warrants a phone call or direct one-on-one communication. Timing is an essential component to mastering great communication. Provide feedback promptly. Be clear and concise. Your communication should be timely and relevant. Be mindful of your audience and ensure that your communication is relevant to all parties you are speaking to. The words you choose to communicate to your employees must be chosen wisely. Speaking down to your employees or using abusive language will not only cause them to lose motivation – it is disruptive to the workplace and is an ineffective tool. The goal is happy, engaged employees.

4 **Leadership** – As we speak about core competencies in regards to acquiring your leadership EDGE, what we have not discussed is the most vital component. That is, are you a leader? At this stage in your career, you know what the title means. You have it. It's part of the fabric of who you are. However, are you demonstrating that you actually are an effective leader. We know that leadership requires a combination of specific skill sets and responsibilities. We understand that we are in a position to make decisions and to guide others. The question then becomes how *exactly* are we doing that? Ask yourself these questions as we progress forward:

Am I, as a leader, demonstrating integrity? Am I visible and easily accessible to staff? Do I hold myself accountable? In my role as leader, do I model positive behavior? Is my behavior consistent? Am I an effective decision maker? Am I influential in a positive way? Do I mentor and help to develop my employees? Do I encourage creativity and participation?

Determining what your leadership style is will lead you in the right direction to gaining your leadership EDGE. What you will find as we progress is not just identifying and defining what the core competencies are, but developing those core competencies in yourself. This isn't a manual that will simply tell you how to expand your knowledge. This book will show you step by step how to take what you know or attain those aspects you didn't possess and to expand upon them and implement them into your daily life.

On the following pages, we will begin to explore and identify your leadership style. When we have a clearer picture of where to begin we will know which path to follow to get you into optimum performance shape.

MY LEADERSHIP QUALITIES

Name _____

On a scale of one to five with five being the highest and one being the lowest circle the best answer you feel reflects you leadership qualities.

Integrity	1	2	3	4	5
Ambition	1	2	3	4	5
Empathy	1	2	3	4	5
Open-mindedness	1	2	3	4	5
Listening	1	2	3	4	5
Credibility	1	2	3	4	5
Energy	1	2	3	4	5
Flexibility	1	2	3	4	5
Trustworthiness	1	2	3	4	5
Adaptability	1	2	3	4	5

Identify my top three leadership strengths.

1._____ 2._____ 3._____

Identify my three weakest areas.

1._____ 2._____ 3._____

What steps do I need to take to strengthen those areas?

_____
_____
_____
_____
_____

Now that we have identified the qualities you believe you possess and you've taken a moment to determine how you can improve on your weaker areas – let's look at common leadership styles and find out which style reflects the kind of manager you are.

The four common leadership styles are:

1. Directive
2. Coaching
3. Influencing
4. Collaborative

DIRECTIVE LEADERSHIP STYLE

The **Directive** leadership style is characterized by having and setting clear goals and rules for your team. You give clearly defined directions that should be easily understood by members of your team. You clarify the tasks and ensure that your team understand their individual roles and responsibilities. Using this style of leadership you would provide guidance and define the criteria for success.

An example of the **Directive** style of leadership would be: A temporary employee is assigned to your team to fulfill a specific task. They, of course, are not familiar with normal procedures and goals. You would give them very specific instructions regarding how to complete the task and you would assign employees that have successfully mastered the job to demonstrate how to accomplish the job.

COACHING LEADERSHIP STYLE

Leaders that choose this style excel at delegating tasks. They identify the strengths and weaknesses of their employees and encourage them to create long-term development goals. These leaders will assign challenging tasks. A positive aspect of using this leadership style is that you, as the leader, are giving continual instruction and feedback. You are taking the time to teach and help that employee or employees to grow. Using this style can raise morale and impact the overall performance of your team. They feel trusted and respected for their hard work and dedication. This style can improve results. The lines of communication must remain open when leading this way. Your job as the leader will be to explain what is expected of the employee and outline how what they are doing has a positive impact on the company as a whole. Using the coaching style tells the employee that you have faith in them and their abilities, thus, creating a more productive employee.

INFLUENCING LEADERSHIP STYLE

This style is all about promoting changes and not just simply managing people or a workforce. As a leader utilizing this leadership style, you can use things like direct appeals to influence your team. There are many different approaches for putting this style of leadership to work for you. We will briefly discuss some options to determine whether or not your style mirrors this particular style of leadership.

- You would provide sound arguments and be able to document evidence or provided documentation of proven evidence for why something is or is not working.
- Set the example.
- Enlist support from persuasive team members
- Remain enthusiastic about your idea.

This approach isn't about using your authority to influence people. It's about influencing people based on your passion or idea and touting the benefits of that idea so that others will want to emulate it. It's not a take no prisoners style. You want a particular result. You design your duties around this approach to get to that result and others may follow suit.

COLLABORATIVE LEADERSHIP STYLE

Collaborative leadership is the premise that when you bring together a group of people to join forces and provide them with good information, they will unite to see that vision through. They will work strategically to get the desired end result. Together they will address the shared problem or concern and collaborate to find a solution.

This style lends to the idea that not one single entity is in charge, per se. Someone, of course, is responsible but there is no clearly defined "boss" on certain tasks. You are all in this together to find a solution or to complete the task.

It is a sort of community effort that leads the team. The leader doesn't make all the decisions. What happens is that the group, or team for our purposes, consider the problem at hand and they make a decision as to what to do about that problem. They present that decision to the group as a whole, then, decide whether or not they will move forward.

Another approach using this style of leadership would be to allow for an open process. That meaning there is no set end point. You work with a goal in mind and continue working until the group as a whole decides that they are done.

Lastly, there is leadership of the process. What this means is that instead of having a specific group, the leader's job will be to keep everyone on task and keep them working towards the aforementioned goal. Someone has to make sure that the team isn't heading in separate directions and that they remain collaborative.

This style of leadership has many advantages. First, it allows for more engagement from the team. It builds trust amongst the team members. It encourages people to take ownership of their efforts and accomplishments. That pride in ownership leads to a deeper commitment to the project and the organization. A final benefit is it eliminates issues regarding being heard as an individual. It provides ample room for establishing mutual trust within the group. Everyone's needs are heard and addressed. Working together in this style puts everyone on common ground. You have created a level playing field for every member of your team.

ASSESSING YOUR LEADERSHIP STYLE

Circle the words in the columns that most strongly match your individual style. When you are done. Count how many you have circled in each column and refer to the scale at the bottom of this page to find out which style most closely reflects yours.

Column One	Column Two	Column Three	Column Four
Control	Listen	Visionary	Team Player
Responsible	Praise	Results Driven	Conscientious
Ambitious	Understanding	Convincing	Considerate
Authoritarian	Empowering	Persuasive	Dependable
Charismatic	Encouraging	Confidence	Sociable
Opinionated	Adaptable	Catalyst	Open minded
Focused	Supportive	Assertive	Sincere

Count the total number of words per column that you circled. The column with the most qualities circled is your preferred leadership style.

Column 1 - Directive Leadership Style
Column 2 - Coaching Leadership Style
Column 3 - Influencing Leadership Style
Column 4 - Collaborative Leadership Style

Recognizing your primary approach to leadership is a tool we can build upon. If you know where your strengths and /or weaknesses are you can formulate a plan that will enable you to build a foundation for success for not only yourself, but success of those around you in the workforce. Understanding where you are lacking in certain areas is the first step in filling in those competency gaps and that will help you to create an action plan to improve in the areas that need the most improvement.

OPTIMIZING DIRECTIVE LEADERSHIP QUALITIES

First we will look at ways to use the Directive Leadership Style to optimize your own potential or if this is not the style you use currently you could learn to incorporate all or some of this style in order to engage those who may not be responding to your current style.

This approach is intuitive, meaning it is easy to learn and implement. You won't need any special skills to begin using aspects of this style in your daily work life. Often you will hear this style referred to as the 'autocratic style'.

The key to this approach is understanding in which situations this would be deemed appropriate. It's better used for high pressure situations when circumstances require someone to take charge and make decisions on the fly. For instance, if a crisis should occur in the workplace, you will need a leader who is authoritative to keep the situation under control and to be able to think on his or her respective feet to ensure that tasks are completed correctly.

In a crisis situation where dangerous work may be involved a leader who is a power house as far as dealing with complicated tasks in a hurry goes must be in charge at all times. There is no time to worry about feelings or emotions. What is critical is whatever that crisis must be.

Another time that this type of leadership may be warranted is not so critical, but important nonetheless. When a new employee comes on board, they will require a lot of direction and close follow up from their leader until they feel comfortable completing their new tasks. Directive Leadership Style would be ideal for this situation.

If there is an employee or employees that are up to par with the tasks or assignments they've been doing for some time, a directive approach may be effective for them. Give them clear directions and ensure they not only are familiar with the overall goal or end result but that they are motivated to see the task through in a timely manner and in the way you implored them to do it.

As a directive leader, you have to be present. You cannot simply bark orders and leave the area. Your follow up is crucial to the teams progression forward. If no one is there to keep them on task and to provide instant feedback, morale will shut down and any hopes of regaining that in your absence will be nullified.

Use what you know. Lead with conviction. Clearly define the roles of your team members. Make yourself available for questions, concerns, and follow ups. Take command especially in crisis situations or when a deadline is looming. Take full responsibility for team decisions. Remain busy. Giving orders and, then, watching others perform those duties without having a function yourself will slow down the entire project. It will dampen the spirits of your team members and cause them to question and doubt your authority. Identify who your strong employees are and don't feel the need to micromanage them using this style. While most will be motivated by this approach, others – like your strongest employees – will feel like they can't be trusted and will not respond well to this approach.

OPTIMIZING COACHING LEADERSHIP QUALITIES

As mentioned previously, coaching style of leadership levels the playing field for everyone on the team. This is ideal when you see the team as people and not just another body in a seat. They should be coached as a team and individually to get them to their full potential.

To begin with you must have a competent and motivated team that has their eyes fixed to the long-term goals of the organization. If their heart is not in it, they will not thrive under this approach. It is your job as the leader to not only emulate enthusiasm and motivation for the tasks at hand but to inspire that in others. Lead by example.

Communication is key for this style of leadership. An effective leader will meet with the group as a whole to gauge their level of commitment. Speak with the them to see what motivates them and find out what their own personal goals may be. Discuss their strengths and formulate a strategy to address their weaknesses. Knowing where the individual began and having an understanding of where they are heading gives you and your organization a competitive advantage.

This approach will build up the individual's confidence and will increase moral because you, as their leader, addressed them as individuals and took the time to work with them and hear their concerns . They will thank you with a higher commitment to the goal and will be anxious to produce better and/or more work. This style will promote excellence among the team members and the team as a whole. It will motivate them to keep turning out good quality work and they will be inspired to continue assessing their job performance and soon will create new and better long-term goals that will benefit not only themselves but the entire organization.

With this in place and continual efforts on your part to assess them at different levels and provide relevant feedback in a timely manner, you will inspire your team members to aspire for more. You are essentially creating future leaders who will in turn do the same for the team they lead. It is a cycle that will remain on an upward swing.

OPTIMIZING INFLUENCING LEADERSHIP STYLE

This approach is best used if you throw any notion of manipulating anyone within your organization into doing anything whether it be good or bad. Approach this style in a way that proves you have an eye toward a mutual goal or benefit. It shouldn't be used to garner favors that benefit yourself or any other individual. For our purposes, we are discussing ethical influencing.

A classic example of an appropriate time to use this approach would be when, for instance, you are called to do some networking or public speaking. You may have some trepidation about this and feel that you are in no way up to this task, but you have someone on your team that is familiar with someone that is well suited to take on this endeavor. Explain your dilemma. Offer sound reasons as to why this may not be right for you cultivate a working relationship with this individual to have them help you network with the qualified person so that you can gain the skills to meet this challenge. What you have done is sought support from someone that can help you carry out what you were called to do.

In the art of persuasion, view your team members as peers and not your prey. Don't set out to take advantage of them or fool them into doing something. Be upfront and honest and explain the situation with the pros and cons. Chances are there will be members of your team that will volunteer to take on the task and will do so successfully and you didn't have to force it on them.

This approach can also be effective when you are in need of someone or some organization to buy-in to whatever initiative you are promoting. (We will discuss buy-in further in the next chapters.) If your intention is to have an individual or a group get behind your idea, you must meet with them first. Going in to a space and trying to harpoon a group of people blindly is ineffective management. Have a plan in place and make it a point to meet with individual members of that group prior to lamenting the pros and cons of your idea or initiative publicly.

If there is an idea or a change you are trying to implement, build a network or a coalition of peers to help you. If a group is working towards one goal together, they are more likely to stand behind that idea or change. They have invested time in it so that alone gives them a sense of pride and they are going to want to stand up for their convictions. Don't go into changes alone if you expect the group to follow. Work as a team and approach the remainder of the organization as team members and not competitors.

OPTIMIZING COLLABORATIVE LEADERSHIP STYLE

Anyone within an organization can be a collaborative leader. This style of leadership is the like the glue that holds the team together. If you remember that analogy, you will be able to effectively utilize this strategy to lead a strong cohesive team. The whole premise with this approach is to work together towards a common goal. The leader must keep in mind that they are not in control in this approach. You must change your mindset and see your team members as peers.

Collectively you brainstorm ideas and solutions and together formulate a plan to get the end result the team decided was the goal. This approach opens up lines of communication and allows you the opportunity to ask questions. It is not your responsibility to know all the answers. As a team you can come up with answers together.

Collaborative efforts allow for creativity to thrive. It will give the chance to see what your team really has to offer. Perhaps, you will find that they have better solutions or more cost effective ways of addressing a problem.

Employees won't feel stifled by leadership. You've eliminated boundaries and they are free to take control as a group. Team work is essential. The team will rise up to the challenge of working with you and not for you and will have a more vested interest in the outcome.

Motivation abounds with this leadership approach. As mentioned, it levels the playing field and allows someone else to shine. You will see who your future leaders and innovators are by allowing them this opportunity to show their skills.

We've discussed the basics of the core competencies and provided real world examples of how these individual approaches can make you a more effective leader. We have touched on morale building and team building. We've defined your preferred approach. Now, we will move on to more precise themes and strategies for success.

CHAPTER II

USING YOUR TIME AND RESOURCES STRATEGICALLY

I THINK WE ALL CAN AGREE that bad time management leads to low productivity and extremely high stress. Both of those things are bad for the team members whom feed off of that stress and bad for the organization that is depending on you to perform your duties in a timely manner and with the utmost of care.

A good leader will lead his or her employees to success by properly utilizing their time and having a set plan in place to make that happen. Proper time management will increase productivity as long as the schedule is adhered to.

What every organization wants and needs in order to thrive is a productive workforce. They expect excellent work. As leaders we have the tools to ensure that's what we produce. How we use those tools is the key to determining if our output is what it should be.

It may have been quite some time since you've been on an interview, but a commonly asked question is how you approach deadlines. Of course, in an interview we provide the most effective response. We would never say deadlines are never met. We typically would answer something along the lines of planning and meeting and exceeding our goals.

Let's take a few minutes to look at and answer time management questions to see where we stand now. Keep in mind, this is for your individual use and since you are already employed in all likelihood providing an honest answer is not going to get you sent out the door. Be honest with yourself and, then, we'll look at ways to improve our time management skills in the workplace.

TIME MANAGEMENT ASSESSMENT

1   If you have 10 tasks for the day and you know you can only complete 5 effectively, how do you determine which one to do first?

_____
_____
_____
_____
_____

2   When you have a huge deadline looming, how do you prepare?

_____
_____
_____
_____
_____

3 With a pile of tasks on your desk to complete, how do you handle interruptions?

_____

_____

_____

_____

_____

The answers you provided to these three questions will help you to identify the areas that you need to work on in regards to time management. Not to worry, as we proceed, strategies that you can begin implementing today will be introduced. Small changes can yield big results.

If management has an effective time management plan in place, their employees will benefit from the example and you will ward off unnecessary stress in the workplace. Remember productivity is key. You cannot be productive if you do not have a way of managing the workflow coming in and the completed tasks going out of your organization.

STEP 1

PRIORITIZE YOUR TASKS

The business world is rampant with interruptions. As the manager or leader it is imperative that you prioritize your work load and manage despite the interruptions, questions, and/or the occasional workplace disaster throughout your day. The key to success when prioritizing tasks is to remain focused on all jobs whether they be large or small.

If you have never worked with a to do list, now would be the time to begin using one. It will give you a working visual of tasks that require your attention and tasks you have completed. You will see your progress and having the ability to physically mark off a task is a motivational tool that has proven successful for many.

First, list all the tasks that require your attention today. Be realistic about what you can actually complete in one day. Rank your list of tasks. If you find that your list is enormously long and seemingly impossible to complete, chance are – you are right.

Now, you will need to whittle that expansive list down to a realistic list of priorities – meaning a list of what absolutely has to be completed today with no exceptions. Having a longer list will discourage you and will work against your productivity goal. The list must be manageable in order for you to be successful.

If items on your list are tasks you know cannot be completed in one day's sitting, break them down into smaller chunks. The goal is to get to done. Slow and steady still wins many races. Think to yourself, in order to get to Part C I need to have accomplished Part A and Part B. Keep this large task on your list if it's a priority. Only you can determine what is and what isn't a priority.

Ask yourself what is important? What job needs to be completed immediately? If a task requires your immediate attention, it must be placed on your list. There are keys to understanding that. Look at all jobs in terms of urgency.

Is the task both urgent and vital to your organizations mission and values? Is it an urgent need, but not necessarily an important one to complete first? If it is neither urgent or important, it doesn't go on the list of tasks for today.

Let's define what urgent and vital means in the workplace. An example would be if there is a malfunction in equipment that your team needs to use otherwise someone may be harmed – that is both urgent and vital. When someone's safety is at stake, that is an urgent situation and must be dealt with swiftly and systems must be put in place to prevent people from coming in harm's way.

If what you deem as urgent and vital is something akin to long-term goal setting or planning with your group – that may not in relation to tasks like the one in the previous example necessarily need to be done today. That task doesn't hinder today's operations.

Look at the bigger picture when formulating your to do list. Is it vital? After looking at the example shown here, compare the tasks you have at hand to that obviously urgent and vital need.

STEP 2

DON'T WASTE TIME

As the leader, take the time to thoroughly explain the task at hand. Give clear directions and answer all pertinent questions the staff may have. Clearly explain your expectations and define how you expect them to accomplish the tasks.

Giving clear directions in the beginning will save you and the team time. There will be no constant interruptions with staff asking for directions and asking questions if you were clear and concise with them initially.

Explain the purpose, the task, the time line, the goal, and how all of these things will impact the organization. If it is important to you or the organization, the staff needs to be made aware of that in order to respond in kind.

Begin your day ready and prepared and show your staff how to do the same. Put a system in place or a plan that walks them step by step through the process of readying their work areas and prioritizing their tasks.

Keep meetings flowing by having something prepared ahead of time. Set a certain amount of time for presentation and another block of time for questions if that is necessary. You do not want to waste hours in never ending meetings while the workload is climbing higher on your desk.

Set realistic expectations. The staff will be more productive if they are not pressured to do more than they can possibly handle in a given time frame.

STEP 3

AVOID PROCRASTINATION

In most cases, fear is the root cause of procrastination. We, as people, are afraid of failure and being judged. When given a task to complete knowing that someone will evaluate that task causes us to fear the results.

As a manager or leader you can combat that fear by looking at the source itself. If your team member procrastinates when the tasks are to be presented to you, could it be because you have not opened a positive dialogue with them? Look at how you have responded in the past. No one is motivated by negative reactions.

If the fear stems from something outside of your potential reaction, find out the source of it and explain the consequences of the action or the consequences if the action isn't carried out as asked. If they know the what, the how, and the why you may have the ability to eliminate their trepidation.

Another common reason for procrastination is not being given clear directions. As leaders we must provide adequate information. If we don't give the team members clear directions, how are we to expect them to complete the vision?

Save yourself and the organization a lot of time by giving the correct information in its entirety and watch your team take the challenge head on with no time wasted.

One reason for procrastination that we also need to consider is the idea that this lack of action is due to bad habit. Have we nurtured an environment that let's procrastination thrive? If that is in fact the case, then, it is going to take some time to reverse that thinking. It's not impossible to conquer.

In this situation, you must change the focus of the group. Again, communication is key. Explain their roles, duties, and expectations with them. Inform them of time lines and explain in detail how what they do plays into the overall set of core values and the mission of the organization. Detail what the consequences of completed tasks are and explain what the consequences of unfinished tasks are and, most importantly, follow through with those consequences.

Help your team to focus on the positive aspects of completing tasks in a timely manner. Don't barrage them with negativity because as mentioned before negativity does not produce results.

STEP 4

DO IT RIGHT THE FIRST TIME

Deadlines are looming. Productivity is down. Reports are do. The clock is ticking. Your workday is almost over. Whatever the reason, we have all at one time or another quickly finished a task in order to go on with our lives or another task and get that off of our desk.

This is ineffective. Chances are your hurrying led to mistakes that could cost the organization money and in all likelihood will cost additional time to correct.

Our role as leader changes as a result of this bad habit. We become 'fixers'. That takes time away from the tasks we have prioritized for our work day.

The reality is we make mistakes when hurrying and sometimes when we are unsure of how to proceed correctly. These mistakes are not solely employee issues. We as leaders make the same mistakes just as often.

To avoid these kind of costly issues, do the job right the first time around. Easy enough it would seem, but let's look at ways to make sure that is how we proceed. Acknowledge that the problem has occurred. Correct whatever the problem or problems are. Decide what needs to be done to avoid having the problem occur again.

Could it be that the work load is unrealistic? Are the tasks too complicated? Are there unnecessary steps? Were you productive all day long or was there a crisis that may have prevented the task from being completed properly? Whatever the reason, address it and formulate a plan to work around those issues or eliminate them altogether.

STEP 5

DELEGATE TASKS APPROPRIATELY

Delegation may be one of the best tools you could use as a manager or leader. If used effectively it could reduce stress overall. You know your staff and you know who is ready to take on new challenges and responsibilities. These challenges could be in relation to answering your emails or filing paperwork or they could be larger projects like supervising and/or monitoring staff. You must first identify who you can trust to complete the tasks and remain confidential and professional. Who are you confident can master this assignment?

Look closely at what they are capable of and decide based on their overall performance and attitude about the job at hand. Give them tasks that complement the skills they've already mastered and/or that will help them grow as individuals. Give them tasks that expand their resumes as a reward.

Delegating doesn't have to be something handed off to one person. You can delegate different relevant tasks to different people on your team. Choose the best ones for the jobs. Look at what they are good at and measure their strong points. Compliment them and explain to them that you chose them based on their abilities and their proven track record.

Delegation of tasks is not given solely to long-term employees. You may find that newer staff may have a better grasp of their job and you may choose them. Delegation isn't about seniority. It is a matter of proficiency and efficiency.

Before assigning new duties to someone speak with them about your expectations and what exactly their roles will be. Like all employees, you must provide clear directions and expectations in order for the workforce to thrive.

Ask them if they are comfortable completing said task. In some cases you may find that a certain task is not appropriate for them and that's okay. People innately want to help out, but respect their right to admit they may not be ready. Don't write them off altogether. You may find that there are other tasks that are more well suited for them and their abilities.

It should be noted that delegation doesn't mean you don't have to monitor or evaluate the work. The responsibility ultimately falls on you as the team leader. If you followed the examples mentioned before of being clear and concise and answering questions and setting limitations and realistic time lines – you will find that delegation is one of the best tools in your leader tool box.

In summary, we will list things that you can do today to use your time more effectively and build a stronger more productive workforce.

KEYS TO EFFECTIVE TIME MANAGEMENT

1. **Be realistic.** – Don't set yourself up for failure with a laundry list of tasks that would be impossible to complete in a reasonable time frame.

2. **Don't overload your team.** - Assign manageable tasks with clear expectations that take their skills and responsibilities into consideration.

3. **Schedule your day including time for breaks and interruptions and mistakes.** - No day goes by without interruption and dilemmas. Allow time for those things. Also, take time to get up and away from your desk to keep the creative juices flowing or to clear your head before you take on the next task.

4. **Define your goals and the goals of the organization.** - Look at long-term goals and short-term goals and see how you can incorporate steps toward completing those goals into your average work day.

5. **Make a to do list every day.** - You have to have a visual reminder of tasks that are both urgent and important to address today. This reminder will motivate you to forge ahead.

6. **Prioritize your duties.** - Decide based on criteria we mentioned what has to be addressed immediately for the safety and well being of individuals or the company at large. Break large tasks into manageable chunks. Determine what is actually urgent and vital today to accomplish.

7. **Do your tasks right the first time.** - Produce quality work each and every time and you can avoid having to go back and redo later.

8. **Communicate expectations effectively.** - Your team is depending on you to lead them. Give them clear and concise directions and clearly state what the positive impact of their compliance will do for them and the organization. Tell them the who, the what, the how, and the why and they will feel respected and will be eager to please you and the organization as a whole.

9. **Delegate appropriately.** - Give tasks to those who are eager, competent, and are proven to have been successful at their job. Don't give more than they are capable of and clearly describe what their new duties are and monitor them to ensure the job is being completed as requested.

10. **Stop procrastination in its tracks.** - Provide clear, accurate information to combat any fear of failure. Information is key to making someone feel comfortable in any given situation. Organize your work day and your work area into production zones. Have a plan to keep yourself focused and moving forward. Know the goals and understand the consequences.

We have addressed time management issues and determined ways to overcome any areas where we are lacking or our employees are lacking. Now we will look at the why we have to manage our time effectively.

An organizations goal is to elicit results. They want a specific outcome as a direct result of the systems they have put in place to garner that outcome. What we call this is Results Focused Plans. What that entails is the consistent delivery of achievable goals. Do you and your team members comply with their quality standards and their service and productivity standards? Do you and your team meet deadlines and do you remained focused on the goal?

Results speak for themselves. If you don't have the tools set in place to get those results, then, we need to help you to build the foundation to achieving those results. Time management was the first priority in building this strong foundation. Now, let's look at these elements and see how you, as the leader, fit into a Results Focused Plan and define areas that you have that may need improvement.

MY RESULTS FOCUSED ASSESSMENT

In terms of yourself, you determine where you will place these categories and, then, we will work on a plan of action to improve areas that need to be addressed.

1. Goal Setting
2. Overcoming Obstacles
3. Quality, Service, and Productivity
4. Solution Focused
5. Follow through

Exceed Expectations	Meets Expectations	Needs Improvements

Now, that you have placed those categories into their respective place on your chart, let's see what these terms actually mean and would your answers change based on these definitions.

1. **Goal Setting** – Set goals that are too easy or too difficult or disregards goals altogether would fall under 'Needs Improvement'. If you establish clear and specific goals, you would fall under 'Meets Expectations'. If you are enthusiastic and meet your goals whether they be simple or difficult goals, then, you 'Exceed Expectations'.

2. **Overcoming Obstacles** – Your effort is lacking and you have no motivation to accomplish the task falls under 'Needs Improvement'. If you find ways to overcome the obstacles and complete the goal, you are under 'Meets Expectations'. If obstacles hinder you in no way, you are under 'Exceeds Expectations'.

3. **Quality, Service, and Productivity** – If you fail to meet quality standards, you 'Need Improvement'. If you take pride in your work and your duties and it shows in your work, you 'Meet Expectations'. If you take pride in your work and the work of others around you and seek out new ways to improve quality and productivity, you are under the 'Exceeds Expectations' category.

4. **Solution Focused** – Giving up or losing focus would put you in the 'Needs Improvement' category. Maintaining focus to get the job done is 'Meets Expectations'. Working diligently to find a great solution if there are problems places you under 'Exceeds Expectations'.

5. **Follow Through** – Doesn't evaluate a solution's effectiveness is 'Needs Improvement'. Checks effectiveness and/or takes action if result is not garnered is 'Meets Expectations'. If you take initiative and continue to try new and innovative solution, you fall under 'Exceeds Expectations'.

Now, having seen the same words in context, do your answers change? Let's fill out the same chart using this new perspective.

1. Goal Setting
2. Overcoming Obstacles
3. Quality, Service, and Productivity
4. Solution Focused
5. Follow Through

Exceed Expectations	Meets Expectations	Needs Improvements

The following is an example of a Results Focused Plan put in place.

LEVEL ONE
The team members understand the job and what their role in accomplishing that job is.

They are focused and able to use the appropriate actions to reach the goal ahead of them.

LEVEL TWO
Employees are able to investigate and challenge their current performance and look at the bigger picture.

Employees have a plan in place to meet challenges effectively.

LEVEL THREE
Employees meet their benchmarks.

Look for and lead results improvement plans and take direct accountability for their performance.

LEVEL FOUR
Use intelligent and relevant measures to plan, lead, and strive for high performance volume.

Embrace changes and challenges and meet them head on.

This is the ideal scenario you want to have in your organization. Happy, competent, efficient employees whom are focused on the overall goal while staying in line with the core values and the mission of the organization they work for.

How we get there is through a systematic approach of eliminating the obstacles as mentioned earlier and formulating a plan of action to take yourself and your team to higher levels of performance and accountability.

We will outline some tools to get your team on the track to success and motivate them to produce more quality results.

ACHIEVING RESULTS
Knowing what results are important and focusing your resources to achieve them.

Create your own measure of excellence.

Use specific methods to garner the outcome you desire. Measure the outcome against a standard of excellence that exceeds the one you have in place.

Make changes within the work methods to improve skills and personal performance.

Contribute to the success of the work unit.

Commit specific resources and time to improve performance

while taking necessary action to   avoid any risks.

Demonstrate a clear understanding of all things contributing to the overall success of your   mission. Look at options and resources readily available to help you succeed.

DEVELOPING BEHAVIORS THAT GENERATE THE DESIRED RESULTS

Create your own measure of success.

Have your team write their own statement about results they are committed to investing their time in achieving.

Develop a performance management plan to gauge the success of your team members with scheduled reviews in place.

Review results regularly either daily or weekly to find areas that may be weak or to see where your plans have successfully contributed to the bigger picture and revise accordingly.

SEEK TO IMPROVE YOUR PERSONAL PERFORMANCE

As the leader, request feedback from your own managers and colleagues and, most importantly,   your team members. If you find that there is a common theme to the feedback, develop a plan to improve in that area. Schedule a follow up review. Use this practice with your team members as well.

If something is not working, rethink it. Brainstorm some ideas to improve the success of your plan.

Put motivating incentives in place. Studies have found that monetary incentives do not   necessarily equate to more productivity or job satisfaction. We will explore this concept more in other chapters. Create your own reward system based on the goals you have accomplished.

MEASURE SUCCESS AS A GROUP

Come together as a cohesive unit and brainstorm successes and failures and craft ideas to either improve or eliminate processes. Use the ideas you generate as a team to develop better options to increase workflow.

Use effective time management skills to schedule the appropriate time to implement any changes after all angles have been studied and everyone has been properly trained on the new concepts or procedures.

DISCUSS HOW YOUR CONTRIBUTIONS LEAD TO SUCCESS

Look at the factors that contributed to success within your organization. What factors contributed to that? Were there other options available? How did that decision effect your organization?

Have discussions with your team discussing those very questions and analyze the results. As a team you will see what works and what does not work. You can base some of your future decisions off of those measurable results.

Discuss with your team in detail how the overall group's performance contributes to the organization. Discuss how your efforts impact the results.

Look at ways you can improve performance now to get better results.

Set reasonable goals to get the most impact from your team's performance.

DEVELOP YOUR STAFF

We discussed the concept of coaching earlier in this book. It is one of the most effective tools you have as a leader. Coaching can help your team in a variety of ways.

- Keeps your team focused.
- Will allow your employees to find ways to improve their personal performance.
- Gives you the opportunity to review their progress on goals and objectives.

- Helps employees understand how what they do contributes to the goals of the entire organization.
- Opens up the lines of communication within the work group.

Development of your staff falls under this same category. Coaching is essentially developing your staff as individuals. It encourages your employees to take their assignments seriously and to tackle them with all the resources made available to them.

Take the time to answer these two questions in depth to measure your own success in the workplace.

- Describe a time when you have done something to improve the performance of your team.

_____
_____
_____
_____
_____

- Describe a time when you have done something that maximized the use of available resources to achieve improved results.

_____
_____
_____
_____
_____

In order to achieve the results your organization desires you must acquire buy-in. How you do that is by using good business sense. Employees rely on you to make transitions smooth. You can ensure a smooth transition by encouraging your team to buy-in to the change.

There are a few simple steps that can lead you to success with a buy-in. Following these steps will save you a lot of unnecessary stress and keep stress at bay for your team members.

First, you must clear lay out the vision for your team. Explain to them what is changing and why that change is necessary for the overall good of the organization. Show them how this change or changes will positively impact their job or career aspirations. Define how you will measure the success of the change to reassure them that the transition will be monitored and someone will follow up on it.

Next, define how exactly the change will affect their current job description or work load. Play to the strengths of your team members. If you give them a task that they can be successful at achieving, they will be more motivated to continue using the new strategy. Be sure that the new goals being set can be measured and have a system in place to hold them accountable for the new expectations. Clearly explain that system to them and how it will affect them.

Lastly, follow up is crucial to maintaining a buy-in. Keep an open door policy to allow as much interaction as possible. There will be inevitable questions and concerns. By showing your team members that you are willing to address their concerns, you will invite them to want to continue on this new path. Also, communication will keep everyone on the same page. Unforeseen challenges may arise and it will be your duty as leader to address those challenges head on and find an amicable solution while keeping the new vision in mind. If the solution you have created doesn't work, allow your team members an opportunity to brainstorm a different solution and make them and their opinion feel valued by implementing their solution if it is appropriate for the task.

Not everyone is going to be receptive to change. Meet resistance head on. If you waffle, it will undermine your authority as the leader of the team. Small problems can lead to much bigger problems. Address the problem of nay sayers before it manifests into a much larger problem that spreads like a venom through the entire team. If that negativity spreads, you will have a tougher time keeping the team members who were on board. Minds could be easily changed if all they are fed is negativity.

As with all things in life, things change. Be prepared to handle a change in the new plan. Nothing is ever set in stone until it is tried and tested and proves to yield the desired results. It may turn out that the change we needed to have the buy-in for does not work after all. Have a plan in place to encourage your team to keep up with the changes and to understand why things are changing again. Get feedback from them about what works and what does not work. Adjust according to what the numbers are saying and what your team members are saying. You will gain respect from them for doing so and they will feel acknowledged and will want to perform their duties well.

Buy-in requires a sense of ownership for the employee. If they don't have a connection to the process or the results, you are not going to have willing participants. Engage staff in performance measurement.

Begin the journey by starting with what your team already knows and build on that by allowing them to learn and discover the advantages of the new change. Initially, people are going to be apprehensive about change. They will fear failure. Build on their strengths and assign them tasks they can complete with success.

Help your team to explore the benefits of the new expectations. Don't just spew information at them and expect them to understand the true impact.

Show your team how to measure their own success and explain how you will measure their success. Respect that they were experts at what they were doing already and keep in mind what kind of results they had been capable of producing. Encourage them to design a new performance measure with these new skills in place.

Encourage your team to seek feedback as individuals and not solely as a team. This shows that you value them independently of one another and will ultimately bring the team closer because it is in our nature to want to help those who may be having difficulty grasping new concepts or theories.

Allow room for their creative energy to thrive. Help them see that the change should not restrict their abilities. They will still have room to seek and find solutions and discover simpler ways to do the work they have been given. Let them have a say in how they will report their successes and/or failures.

When a change has been put in place, don't micro-manage your employees. Allow them time to explore and become familiar with the new concepts. Intervene when prompted to, but don't hover and cause friction where there doesn't have to be any. Set aside time to reflect with each of them individually to discuss their job performance and answer any questions or concerns they may have as a result of the changes.

Follow up with the team members regularly while the changes are going into effect. Too many things will begin to backlog and allowing too much time in between evaluations and assessments could harbor resentments and will destroy the ability to attain a successful buy-in from the employees. Your proverbial door must remain open for questions and concerns. If time doesn't allow for regular interruptions, inform your team members exactly when you will be available for questions or provide an avenue with which they can communicate with you and give them a specific time line for when their concerns will be addressed. Having them send emails that you never respond to is bad business and in order to attain and maintain a buy-in your team members must be respected and feel that they are making a real contribution to the overall outcome of the project or projects they are working on at the time.

These steps may not be the only way to garner a buy-in, but they are a way that can lead you on the path to a successful buy-in. Believe that overall most people want to contribute and they will help if what you are offering is realistic and has systems in place to measure their successes and their contributions to the bigger picture. Allow time to reflect with the team members individually and as a group. Actively listen to concerns. Answer questions promptly. Pro

CHAPTER III

GATHER AND SHARE INFORMATION EFFECTIVELY

COMMUNICATION LINKS ALL FACETS of the corporate world together. Having effectively communication allows for a better experience for all. Corporate goals and objectives may give direction to the marketing team, the production crew, finance department, personnel, and maintenance but communication links all of those facets to organizational success. In order to maintain effective functioning in the workplace, effective communication is essential. Not only should managers and leaders practice communication, but all employees must strive to maintain an atmosphere conducive to communicating with success.

As leaders one of your roles is to help your team – your employees – improve their communication skills. When every member of a team or an organization is on the same page as far as communication is concerned, everyone is more likely to perform well. A successful leader/ manager needs to practice effective communication themselves in order to inspire it in their employees.

To gather a basic understanding of the concept of effective communication, let's break down what it means and, then, we will look at how to apply it to our everyday lives. At its most basic, it is the sharing of information within a group of two or more that allows them to reach a common understanding. What is crucial to that basic understanding is that the message or ideas were conveyed in terms and phrases that the entire group thoroughly understands. To see an example of this in practice, take a moment to consider when you have either given or received incomplete information and ponder what the results of that failure in communication were. Partial understanding of a term or concept is not enough to be able to make a sound decision with. All parts must be communicated effectively to garner the outcome we expect.

A myth shared by many about communication is that agreement translates to understanding. That is one issue that needs to be addressed clearly. Consent without knowledge of or a clear understanding of the task at hand is not an example of effective communication. On that same note of myths in communication, we as leaders sometimes fail to realize that when a member of our team or coworker disagrees with our decisions or directives that it must mean the person does not completely understand our point. That is simply not true. A person can completely disagree with your point or your decision *and* have a clear understanding of what you have communicated to them. Understand that you each may fully understand the other's position, but that doesn't have to result in agreement.

We can split communication into two distinct phases:

— the transmission phase
— the feedback phase

In the first – the transmission phase – information is sent from one person or group (the sender(s)) to another person or group (the receiver(s)).

To begin a transmission phase, the sender(s) decide which message to send. That message is the information the sender wishes to communicate to the receiver(s). The sender translates the message into language sent through a chosen pathway (phone call, email, text message, etc.) and that message is transmitted to the receiver(s).

In the feedback phase the receiver becomes the sender and initiates communication. The receiver decides which message to send to the original sender and transmits that message through a chosen pathway (phone call, email, text message, etc.) to the original sender who is now the receiver. This particular message may contain a confirmation of receipt of the original message or a restatement of the original content to clarify what was said or it may contain a request for additional information.

There are many forms of communication that must be addressed as well. We are familiar with the term nonverbal communication, but let's look at it closely to determine what messages we may be sending to our team members.

Nonverbal communication shares information through body language, facial expressions, and gestures. Nonverbal communication can also be conveyed by physical elements like structures and buildings and their furnishings. How often have you entered a building and noticed the décor and made a decision as to what kind of place it was based on that décor? How furniture or offices are arranged conveys messages regarding status, prestige, power, and influence.

Notice your body language as you talk with people. What messages could your body language be sending? Are you closed off with arms crossed in front of you? Are your shoulders slumped in defeat? You may not have noticed simple things like that, but in all likelihood those around you have noticed.

Learn to align your verbal messages with your nonverbal messages. An example of that would be when congratulating a team member for a job well done – look them in the eye, smile, stand straight and proud. Expressions such as that will ring true and make your remarks that much more sincere and appreciated.

How your messages are received are a matter of perception. Nonverbal messages can undermine what your verbal messages are meant to convey. Your message can be taken out of context and be deemed as something it is not. Your cues and signals are easily misunderstood.

Perception is a personal process by which people organize and interpret sensory input to give meaning and organize the world they live in. It is highly subjective and can be influenced by values, attitudes, moods, personal experience, personality, and knowledge base. When you send or receive a message, you are doing so based on your own subjective perceptions.

Prior to communicating one should determine by which means would be the most effective way of conveying their message. Not all situations call for the same type of communication channel. Some channels may be more appropriate than others and some may not be good choices in the business world. Let's explore your communication options one at a time.

Face-to-face communication – As a leader, you understand that most of your time is spent one-on-one with your team or employers. That is what face-to-face communication is. It's speak one-on-one to someone and allows them to provide immediate feedback and is probably the best method for communicating when compared to the other forms of communication we will discuss. The reason it is deemed the best is because it allows room for several channels of communication to be interpreted including: voice, eye contact, body language, and small gestures. This form of communication is ideal for leaders and managers when they are delegating tasks, giving instructions, disciplining an employee, answering questions, coaching a team member, or checking on the progress of an assignment. Using one-on-one (face-to-face) communication helps you as the leader develop and maintain good interpersonal relations with your team members and your colleagues.

Written Communication – It is difficult to convey a feeling or a clear message via a written communication. Words on a page can be easily misinterpreted and tone may be improperly potentially causing bad feelings. It also impedes the feedback process as feedback may take exceptionally long to return if at all. When you are addressing a group of people using written notes or messages, you are in a sense derailing their ability to cohesively understand your message and you are not allowing your message to be focused which is key to effective communication. This type of communication would be the least valuable to you in the workplace.

Telephone Communication – Communication via the telephone limits the amount of full communication the receiver could receive. It only allows them to receive voice inflection cues and doesn't give them the added benefit of visual cues like in face-to-face communication. In order to communicate effectively over the phone, an ample amount of time must be dedicated to every exchange and this is not conducive to a productive work day. Eight hours simply doesn't afford much time to provide detailed descriptions and explanations over the phone. While it may be convenient, there are some items you must acknowledge prior to picking up the phone – set a clear objective, write down a list of exactly what you'd like to say or discuss, have a pen and paper ready to take notes (if necessary), set aside enough time to allow for adequate explanations and feedback. You may use this form of communication to save time in a pinch, but never use it for detailed directions or any disciplinary actions.

Technology – We all know it. We all use it. The question we will answer is whether or not the use of technology is effective in the workplace? What the use of technology has done is that it has increased the speed of communication. That's a given. It affords you the opportunity to communicate more easily with your team members and you can receive prompt feedback. That's great for business. In order to remain competitive, you must use all of the exciting advancements and tools. But you should not adopt the practice of using them without carefully considering whether or not it is actually improving overall performance and is improving the workflow. One giant pitfall with the immediacy of technology in the workplace is the fact that you may initiate a response that seconds later would be deemed inappropriate. Meaning, let's say, you received a message that Team Member A completed a large project and it's ready to be turned in. You immediately convey that message to your superiors or client and seconds later Team Member A alerts you to a major problem that requires reckoning immediately. Now, you must turn around and apologize and explain to your superiors or the client that the original message may have been sent prematurely. You see the problem with immediacy of information here? Bottom line, by all means, use all that technology has to offer but don't do so without making sure there are systems in place for situations like the one in our example. Have all the facts and know exactly what it is you should communicate and how at any given time.

Personality Types in Communication

We all follow under a certain personality type when it comes to our way of communicating. We explore these types and allow you to discover which type you are, what the strengths and weaknesses are, and how you can use that to help you in your communication with your employees. Understand that most of us have a dominant personality type and one or two secondary personality types. These, like us, evolve over time. Each of the personality types we will discuss has two distinct facets that must be considered as well. One is a higher maturity level that generally allows us to succeed and mature in life and in our professional careers. The other is a lower maturity level that typically suffers from persistent problems at home and at work.

The Helpful Nurturers – These people tend to be very nice, supportive, sensitive, and friendly.

The Creative Idealists – They tend to be motivating, fun, persuasive, and energetic.

The Cerebral Realists – Tend to be task driven, analytical, and very detail oriented.

The Strategic Directors – These people tend to be powerful, controlling, productive, and   conscious of achievements.

The Helpful Nurturers possess these common traits: sociable, subjective decision-making, conduct is based on values and intuition. Pitfalls for them may be that their personal feelings can get in the way of their objectivity. At times, they may come off as being passive and have difficulty saying no. These traits are a clear indication that this personality type may be ineffective when it comes to communication because they may be unable to clearly offer constructive criticism or convey the exact message they should because they are concerned with causing hurt feelings. The nurturers want to be liked and accepted. If this personality describes you, find ways to get that feeling of appreciation without jeopardizing your ability to communicate effectively. Understand that there is a job to be done and that everyone including yourself will be much more satisfied with a job well done than with a job done only to appease someone's sensitive nature. As a leader, when challenges come up, stress that the issue does not affect the quality of their overall work. Speak warmly and thank your team for their efforts and clarify what exactly the expectations are and what deadline has been set in place to meet those expectations.

The Creative Idealists are imaginative, insightful, and very subjective. They are motivated by uncovering the meaning and overall significance of things around them. We are all familiar with the term self-actualization. That is what the creative idealists craves. For them, it is about evolving and working towards becoming what they believe they should. How that plays into communication is that the idealist is especially skilled at persuading one to do something. Talking is their forte. They are wonderful motivators and can easily get their team to follow their lead. One could say they are intuitive communicators because they are extremely sensitive to small changes in gestures and behavior that other personality may not pick up. They also tend to be prone to the use of metaphors which could be misinterpreted in the workforce. For instance, "You are such an angel" or the "sun shines on you". Albeit, these two phrases are kind there are a number of phrases which may be deemed as off-putting and have no place in the office. Written communication for the idealist tends to be quite lengthy and extremely detailed as this personality type thrives on the use of words and the desire to communicate wholly. Ideally, leaders with this personality type are best suited for teaching new processes or for training new hires and are extremely effective at taking notes and writing manuals and instructions. They are a passionate breed who can draw from their very special talents to lead a highly engaged team.

The Cerebral Realists are task driven, analytical thinkers who tend to be quiet and reserved in the workplace. Curiosity is their strongest motivator. Their intellect is sharp and their interest lies in the fundamental nature of things. How these traits impact communication is that they tend to not be interested in sharing their findings or reasoning with others. They like to work alone and thrive on clear concentration. You can imagine what that personality type could do in a group setting. It is one thing to be independent and self-reliant, but not at the expense of the team as a whole. Take a look at these terms associated with this personality type and determine if any of these apply to you.

— introverted
— theoretical
— rational
— pensive
— self-involved

Learning to let go of some of your tight control and allow the opinions of others to play a role in the decision-making process is a skill that must be learned for the cerebral realists. Their independent nature may be misconstrued as arrogance in the workplace. Again, communication strongly relies on perception and cerebral realists need to remember that when they are leading a team. Be mindful of your body language and allow yourself to open up and have one-on-one conversations even if the opinions vary greatly from your own. You will gain respect and will find a new appreciation for those whom you lead every day.

The Strategic Directors are born leaders that embrace change and are highly goal-oriented. They thrive on competition. Where their weaknesses lie is in that they tend to be impatient and tactless and come on strong. All of those and more lead directly to ineffective communication. These quick tempered directors leave those in their employ frustrated and sometimes fearful. Although direct, brief, to the point answers are what the Strategic Director wants, at what overall costs are they getting it? Your job as a leader is not to intimidate your employees. Your job is to encourage and provide an environment in which they can grow and thrive. One tool these types can use to create a more clear channel for communication is to outline what it is they require and to provide that outline to their team members so there is no question as to what is expected. Agree as a team (yourself included) how time lines and sanctions will be communicated and dealt with if a they are not carried out. Do not bully your team. Stress the logic of your ideas. Stick to business discussions only. Never comment on anything not directly related to work.

You have had an opportunity to see clear examples of the different personality types in communication. It is now up to you to pull winning aspects from the varied types and formulate a strong, effective type with which you can garner the exact results you'd like. While some of the four we discussed may be seen as clearly wrong, there are aspects of each that do speak to the overall success of any business setting and with imagination and determination can be incorporated into your work life to provide the most effective communication option for yourself and for the members of your team. In the end, everyone will have a more pleasant experience and will follow your example and will utilize the tools you emulate by communicating effectively with one another.

CHAPTER IV

HOW TO TRANSFORM EMPLOYEES INTO OWNERS OF THE ORGANIZATION'S SUCCESS

EMPLOYEE EMPOWERMENT is a key factor in transforming a good employee into an owner of the success of the organization at large. It is the strategy or philosophy, if you will, that enables those on your team to make sound decisions about the jobs that they do and how they will continue to perform. This strategy empowers employees to work independently and to take full responsibility for the results they achieve.

This philosophy authorizes each team member as an individual the opportunity to think on their own, take action, exhibit behaviors conducive to meeting a collective and/or individual goal, to have some control over the work they do, and have some decision-making power over their work. Inevitably, they will feel self-empowerment and have the ability to control where their efforts take them in the workplace.

The level of responsibility you as the manager/leader choose to impart on your employees is a decision you must make based on abilities and other factors you will deem appropriate for the job at hand. The decisions these individuals are empowered to make can be large or small depending on the task to be done and the level of responsibility you as the manager choose to assign.

Take into consideration factors including:

- the nature of the work you do
- the environment in which you work
- what's the level of skill needed for the work
- is there a time line for the work to be completed
- is there a set plan in place to complete the work – a structure

In order for a leader to foster employee empowerment, they must first ensure their individual trait's promote employee empowerment. There are a number of traits an effective leader must have in order to assign responsibility in the correct manner.

Below is a list of the desired traits for a manager/leader to possess:

- Listen to your employees. Hear them effectively.
- Communicate effectively and in a timely manner.
- Show respect for yourself and your employees.
- Be accountable and expect that your employees take accountability for their actions.
- Don't take credit for what the employees have done.
- Have a positive attitude at all times.
- Delegate tasks effectively.
- Be clear and concise when giving instructions.

- Recognize, acknowledge, and celebrate the achievements of your employees.
- Maintain an open door policy. (Communication!)
- Welcome and invite feedback from employees.
- Not only must you know their job, but you must be able to do their job. (You can't teach what you don't know.)
- Promote employee education and training.
- Give out power responsibly. You are still accountable for their work. Don't depend on them to do your work.

One might ask how empowerment would benefit the organization as well as the individual. We've already outlined some key factors for employees. Let's look at some often forgotten or hidden benefits of empowering employees in respect to what that may mean for the organization.

The empowerment process can have a major impact on the profitability of an organization. If you, as the leader, are using your resources effectively and, thus, giving power to the employees to do the same – you can control the number of resources used and control the bottom line of the organization.

Effectively tapping into the potential of the individual members of your team will benefit the company as a whole in tremendous ways. Not only will you have happier employees but you will increase their productivity and they will work more efficiently because now they have a stake in the results and can take full responsibility for their efforts.

Another benefit that often goes unnoticed is the idea of employee turnover and absenteeism. If an employee does not feel valued for the work that they do and their efforts to get that job done, they will lose any motivation to continue producing quality results for that company. Acknowledging their contributions and their efforts regularly – if not, daily – and striving to make them feel empowered to make decisions in the workplace will give them the incentive to go to work every day and to be more productive and take pride in their work.

If each member of an organization is treated as you would expect to be treated and respected for their efforts, the group as a whole begins to work cohesively to meet a common goal and that path they take together serves as a built-in incentive to not let themselves, their peers, or the organization down. They won't seek out other positions or organizations because they are valued where they are and, in the end, the company saves money that allows them to continue to hire and train new employees and promote those who are succeeding from within.

What most leaders have difficulty understanding is that employees have a wide range of discretion regarding how much or how little effort they will make. If the employees are empowered they will be motivated to increase their efforts and will be more open to contribute ideas and concepts that may improve other factors in the workplace.

The purpose of creating an empowered workforce is to foster employee commitment. That is the goal. Your role as leader is to ensure that everyone on the team has the same mission and goals. That includes you. Do your actions match what you have said and done? Are they consistent with what you expect of your employees? If not, it is imperative that you correct any failings and begin to be a beacon of change for not only your employees, but for yourself and the organization. You will see better results once you are fully vested in the process.

We ask a lot of our employees. Goals change daily. Systems change. When we assess how the employees feel or define a situation. Do we ask those same questions of ourselves? Next, we will quiz ourselves in terms of how empowered we feel in the workplace. Once we can define empowerment in relation to our personal feelings, then, we can better assess how empowered members of our team feel.

EMPOWERMENT ASSESSMENT

1. Are you encouraged to improve, learn, and grow as an employee/ leader?

_____

2. Do you have all of the equipment, tools, or resources needed to fulfill your duties?

_____

3. Do your managers/leaders maintain an open door policy for communication?

_____

4. Do you feel that upper management and team members value you and your efforts?

_____

5. Is your role clearly defined?

_____

6. Are your goals clearly articulated?

_____

True or False

Managers must accept responsibility for their decisions and be able to justify their actions.

- **True**
- **False**

Empowerment creates discontent in the workplace.

- **True**
- **False**

Learned helplessness is a key component utilized in the empowerment philosophy.

- **True**
- **False**

Take the time to evaluate the questions and answers on the Empowerment Assessment. Your feelings will help you to understand what your team members feel and want. If you don't feel that your contributions are valued, you have to ascertain how your employees may feel.

To build on what we already have learned, we will look at collaboration and how that contributes to the overall theme of employee empowerment.

COLLABORATION

Collaboration in the workplace is the harnessing of the collective brainpower within an organization. We often rely on our own knowledge and motivations to sustain us in the workplace. The idea of empowering employees says that when employees take ownership in the process and the results, they begin to work cohesively to meet a specified goal. Collaboration is the glue that makes that process stick together. Working collaboratively could potentially save an organization billions of dollars and keep the company in business for many years to come.

As leaders, creating an environment that is inclusive will energize the team and their increased productivity will dramatically impact the bottom line not only for your discipline or area, but for the entire organization. Collaboration is an issue that leaders must focus their attention on. In order to be successful, a leader must recognize where their team's weaknesses are and model a change in attitude and behavior that inspires others to follow suit.

In order to succeed at making that change, a leader must recognize that you need the team to work with you – it's a group effort that will make a difference. The team cannot be successful unless each of them feels the impact of the change from start to finish. Results speak volumes in regards to continued motivation. Change is best made as a team and not as a rogue employee with no support.

There are 3 concepts to keep in mind in order to create a more collaborative workplace:

- Communication
- Acknowledge
- Visualization

We have discussed Communication and Acknowledging at length in previous chapters. Let's examine the concept of Visualization. We are familiar with defining what it is we'd like to achieve and where we'd like to go, but in terms of collaboration, there is another part of visualization to consider.

In an effort to work together toward the defined common goal, every member of the team must be able to clearly see what the desired outcome or result is. How we can make sure that the employees see that is by the use of visuals to effectively communicate your ideas and to clarify ideas for them. It goes to the concept of learning modes. Some people gather information through auditory cues, others may be more tactile, while others – as in the concept of visualization – may need to actually see what the goal is. That can be in the form of photos of a finished product or component or the use of prototypes of models. Charts showing desired results and clear steps to get to that goal are another very effective visual that can be provided. Leaders have used power points to get an idea across. It has been proven that visuals are six times more effective than words alone. If the entire group can see the process or the concept, they will have another tool to guide them to success as a team.

ESSENTIAL COMPONENTS OF TEAM DEVELOPMENT

Tannebaum and Schmidt (1958) and Sadler (1970) developed a model that is still in use today that applies to building a strong, empowered team. Their discovery leans toward a continuum of progression that garners the desired results. It is, as follows:

- **Tell** – Leaders make a decision and announce that decision to the team with complete clarity and the team follows those directions exactly as given.

- **Sell** – Leaders make the decision and then try to sell or get the employees to buy-in to the concept by detailing all of the positive components and benefits to the team members.

- **Consult** – Leaders invite team members to provide input, but maintain full authority and are the final decision makers.

- **Join** – This is an example of empowering the employee. The leader invites the team members to provide input and have the power to make the final decision.

As the leader, the level of employee involvement is dependent upon the needs of the organization, your knowledge of that person's skills and/or experience, their ability to completely understand the concept, plan, or instructions. It's the same model used when you choose to delegate a job. Is this the right person for the job? Is this the right job for this person? It is all a matter of how well you actually know your employees and their capabilities.

TEAM BUILDING PROCESS
A strong team must have a strong leader. The most effective leaders have created an environment of trust and loyalty and make an effort to build relationships and harness creativity. Ruling with fear and intimidation is a sign of weakness and not power. Below are things to consider and incorporate into your team building process:

- Communicate clearly.
- Encourage an environment of trust and team work.
- Facilitate communication.
- Communicate the ground rules and parameters for the team and for everyone individually.
- Delegate tasks accordingly. Allow room for problem-solving among the team.
- As a team, set goals or objectives.
- Solve problems as a team.
- Value your employees and their ideas.

- Recognize visual clues such as body language and demeanor.
- Encourage team discussions and brainstorming sessions.
- Maintain an open door policy.

Utilizing all of these concepts makes you a stronger, more effective leader and creates an environment that every employee will be happy to be a part of and increases their dedication to not only the task at hand, but the job, and the mission of the organization.

ROLES TEAM MEMBERS PLAY

Teams that work together toward the same goal can have a lasting impact on the organization and the group dynamics. The list of roles team members play touches on every aspect of the company's success and mission and values. Leaders will want to take note of all of the different ways in which a strong team can make an enormous difference overall.

The team will:
- Empower individuals and the organization.
- Work together to achieve objectives.
- Generate new and innovative ideas.
- Increase job satisfaction.
- Hold team members accountable for their actions.
- Allow team members to feel valued.
- Build trust and strong work relationships.
- Use knowledge to improve services and products for the organization.
- Encourage communication among team members.
- Provide a place to share information and combine resources.
- Build future leaders.
- Provide an opportunity to apply multiple perspectives and views.

FACTORS WHICH CONTRIBUTE TO WINNING TEAMS

1. **Leadership** – Every team needs a strong, focused leader. A strong leader is committed to the team's results and holds individuals responsible consistently for their actions. The leader must have a

system in place to monitor and evaluate the efforts of the group and those of each of the team members individually. Leadership above all else has the strongest impact on the success of the team.

2. **Shared Vision** – The team must be on the same page and hold the same interest and values. They must work together to solve problems, develop ideas, identify things that work and things that don't work, and have identified the goal or goals that they are striving for.

3. **Commitment** – The collective membership of the team is what is needed to gain success. If there is no commitment to the goal or the objective and the attitudes work against the vision, the goals won't be met. It's a self-fulfilling prophecy. If they aren't committed to it, chances are they won't make an effort to strive for it.

4. **Trust** – Teams thrive on trust. If the team is not made to feel that they can openly object or dispute a concept or feel that their opinions don't matter, they won't be interested in helping the team meet their goal. Teams must be able to know and understand their team members and the opinions or ideas belonging to those team members.

5. **Collaboration** – Every team member must be actively involved in the process. They will take ownership in their efforts. They will be committed to the goal of the group. As a whole, each member will be more actively engaged. Working together changes the dynamics of the team. They will focus on goals, issues, or problems as a group and can brainstorm ways to solve or combat those issues.

PUTTING TEAM BUILDING THEORY INTO PRACTICE

We are familiar with the general concept of building a team. However, there are a number of different versions as to how to implement the theory. In general, team building approaches fall into three separate categories.

1. Group activities like competitions or team sports.
2. Matching personality or work styles.
3. Group analysis and discussions.

While categories one and two are self-explanatory. Three may be unfamiliar. Let's take a look at what it consists of.

- Understanding the workload and assigned tasks.
- Coordinating regular group activities throughout the year.
- Work together to develop new approaches.
- Assist one another in tasks.
- Establish both long-term and short-term goals for the group.
- Identify ways in which staff can become more efficient.

DETRIMENTAL EFFECTS OF INTERNAL COMPETITION

Pitting employees against one another either by way of reward or points is one of the most ineffective motivation tools used by companies worldwide. While it can be said that a little healthy competition is good – rewards and recognition solely based on a sales number or production number should not be used in the workplace.

In order to master a skill, competition doesn't have to be part of the picture. Goal setting and skill mastering should be based on clear, fair practices. It is a failure of competition to insinuate that faster performance or higher volumes equates to superior work output. Faster is not always better.

Overall performance of a group can increase exponentially if their leader or leaders not only expect, but verbalize that they expect the group to do well. In essence, 'talking up' a project or a job will work as a self-fulfilling prophecy for the group. They will believe that they can do it and they will do it. This idea is what is termed the 'Pygmalion effect. The dictionary defines this as, "the phenomenon whereby the greater the expectation placed upon people, the better they perform." (Terence R. Mitchell and Denise Daniels: Motivation (2003). Walter C. Borman, Daniel R. Ilgen, Richard J. Klimoski, ed. Handbook of Psychology, volume 12. John Wiley & Sons, Inc. p. 229. ISBN 0-471-38408-9.)

Every leader has a set of expectations in their mind. Voice those expectations in a positive light and be mindful of your nonverbal cues. Your body language must mirror the message you wish to convey.

Utilize positive employee recognition strategies. That's not to say that you shouldn't single out someone who has done well. Always acknowledge achievements. The key is not to do so in the form of competition. Just as there is stress anxiety – there is anxiety associated with having to compete with one another for accolades or rewards.

ACHIEVING ORGANIZATIONAL GOALS

With extensive interaction and coordination between all parties within a department you can achieve your organizational and leadership goals. Policies and programs must be put into place that enable the team as a whole to clearly understand what their objectives are and know exactly how they will reach their set goals. Resources must be made available so that they can perform the duties required of them. Performance goals must be created and agreed upon by most if not all parties involved. A system of checks and balances must be implemented and utilized on a regular basis to ensure that the system put in place is effective and moving the group closer to their collective goals.

The primary goal of management should be to develop organizational goals and to make logical and reasonable decisions. All functions should be organized in a way that makes sense to the group. All employees must be motivated to work together effectively to achieve the organizational goals.

Planning, communicating, leading, and controlling are key factors that coincide with every step of the process. The manager must oversee the day to day performance of their team members and follow up with them in a timely fashion with constructive remarks that build up the employee and motivates the employee.

In summary, working together to achieve approved goals and respecting the opinion of others while motivating through positive feedback and direct communication is the key to success of the team as a whole. People are motivated by those who emulate confidence and exude a winning attitude.

CHAPTER V

ENHANCE JOB OWNERSHIP AND PERFORMANCE

WHEN KEY FACTORS TO EMPLOYEE SATISFACTION are addressed, job performance will enhance. Bearing in mind that this responsibility does not fall entirely on your employees or team members. Like all of the other points we've discussed in earlier chapters, leaders must emulate the behaviors they wish to see. Leaders have to create an environment within their organization that inspires their employees to want to enhance their own job performance. To begin, we will outline steps to improve job performance.

- **Get organized.** Rid your office, desk, and/or cubicle of clutter. If there is an item that is rarely or never used, clear it off of your desk. Rid your area of the mountains of sticky notes attached to every surface. If they contain valuable or pertinent information, create a file for them on your desktop that you can open whenever necessary. They do not need to take up space in your work area. A cluttered space is the equivalent of a cluttered mind. Evaluate your area. Is it counterproductive? Are you finding that in order to perform a function or duty, you are having to maneuver around your area to get that one thing done? If so, you are defeating any chance of being productive. Too many steps to perform one function detracts from your productivity. Use the LEAN method. We will discuss the LEAN method further later in this chapter.

- **Prioritize your projects or duties.** As discussed before, create lists of priorities. What needs to be addressed immediately? Look at the amount of time you are spending to fulfill those duties. Are you spending enough time or too much time addressing those issues? Is something you are doing getting in the way of your productivity? Create a file system that works for you not against you.

- **Develop new habits.** If you make it part of your daily routine to leave your work area clean and organized, you will have a built in system allowing you to be more productive each and every time you return to your work area. You'll find that you won't be wasting valuable time setting your area up for the next task. It's done and ready to go. Take a few minutes at the end of every shift to file items that may need to be filed, to trash items that don't need to be kept, to put supplies and tools in their proper spaces, add any pertinent information scribbled on scratch pads or notes into the file you created on your desktop. Get in the habit of using a personal organizer system that works for you not against you. If what works for you is a notebook, then, by all means, use a notebook. If you are a techy, use any of the many systems available online to keep you and your work all in one place. Anything that you won't have time for an realistic amount of time, move to the next workday's to do list. Lastly, make sure you allow time off for yourself. You need time off to rejuvenate and energize. Have family time. Do the things that make you happy.

- **Manage every minute of your day.** This step is not meant to add stress to your already busy life. What this step is about is planning. Don't go into a project without knowing how you will accomplish the task. Or, don't conduct a meeting blindly. Plan the topics you will discuss. Work is not the place that you want to live 'by the seat of your pants'. Work is the place that you want to know exactly what you are doing in order to be more productive.

WHAT IS LEAN?

Lean is the philosophy that encourages the maximizing the time by minimizing the steps necessary to complete a project. As mentioned, too many steps defeats the purpose of being productive. Lean is about optimizing the flow of product. Eliminating waste within an entire organization increases the overall productivity. Focus on the entire process.

This process of increasing productivity by minimizing steps applies in every business. Leaving behind the notion of saving money. This process alters the way of thinking and acting within an entire organization. Analyze each step your team makes and brainstorm ways to make the process more efficient. Small steps can make huge changes. For instance, are your employees having to get up and walk away from their stations to perform any part of their duties? Perhaps, move parts that can be moved. That alone can shave minutes off of the time it takes to complete a process, thus, making your employees more productive.

APPLYING 5S LEAN PHILOSOPHY

This philosophy is a structured method to organize any workplace environment. 5S is the pillar of Lean philosophy. This system captures the core principles of the Lean philosophy and will facilitate the development of a Lean system that lasts. These principles are your foundation on which you build your Lean process. This is the beginning of building a new environment that enables the pursuit and elimination of waste from your organization.

1. **Sort** – Keep only necessary items in your workplace.
2. **Set in order** – Arrange items to promote efficient workflow.
3. **Shine** – Clean the work area so it is neat and tidy.
4. **Standardize** – Set standards for a consistently organized workplace.
5. **Systematize** – Maintain and review standards.

5S IN PRACTICE

- **Sort**: Separate the items you will need for the job from the items you don't need. Examples include obsolete and expired procedures, damaged or expired inventory, old equipment, broken equipment. After sorting, discard unneeded items.

- **Set in order:** For those items that you will need, put them in logical order or place in a convenient, logical place to enhance workflow and reduce chance of injury or damage. The order items are placed in should contribute to the reduction in excess movement and excess delays. There are 7 waste lean methods that can be eliminated in an organization. (excess movement, excess transportation, over processing, over production, excess inventory, excess delays, and defects)

- **Shine** – The work area is clean and the equipment and systems are calibrated to ideal settings for the process. At this point, the measurement of the system can begin and you will be able to capture any variation in the process.

- **Standardize** – While there may be many ways to do a job, there can only be one best way. Collaboration can help you identify the best way to complete a task. That way should be the standard. Everything from the actual task to how to replenish or manage inventory.

- **Systematize** – Put into place a system to maintain the organization of the workplace such as monitoring the upkeep of equipment, measuring results, maintaining visual control of the process. Applying a feedback and response system that is consistent.

UNDERSTANDING EMPLOYEES NEEDS

We have discussed in depth the roles employees play within an organization. Now, let's break that down even further and make it much more personal. Granted the people you lead and/or manage are your team members or your employees but first and foremost they are human beings and they have needs. Yes, their needs relate to the workplace as well. Most of us are familiar with Maslow's Hierarchy of Needs. We've heard discussions in high school or in a lecture during college. Being familiar doesn't equate to thoroughly understanding what these needs may be. Finding out a person's needs, capabilities, and aspirations and addressing those items can have a meaningful impact on productivity.

The basics of these individual needs are physiological needs, safety needs, social needs, ego, self-actualization. While we are familiar with those, we may not readily be able to see how those apply to the individuals that work with or for you and we may not know how to respond to those needs within the workplace. Let's examine some key points:

MOST EMPLOYEES WANT TO:
- be acknowledged and rewarded
- realize their ideals
- be able to advance
- earn a good wage
- improve their skills and knowledge
- demonstrate and utilize their talents

EMPLOYERS CAN RESPOND TO THEIR NEEDS BY:
- offering employment
- providing adequate pay (a fair wage)
- providing a stable work environment
- rewarding and recognizing employees who deserve accolades
- offering training and development programs
- assisting employees with their personal needs (child care incentives, transportation, flexible work schedules)
- providing an atmosphere of teamwork and cooperation

Plan company policies bearing in mind that your employees are people who have responsibilities outside of work. Consider their family responsibilities when scheduling. They may have heavy financial burdens. Although, you don't need to know the particulars, understand that a regular paycheck with regular hours is something employees count on and need to keep their families afloat. If a desperate financial need is called to your attention, answer to that. Are there additional projects or hours to be offered? Look at ways in which you could help.

One aspect to consider is not only that your employees have needs, they also have certain expectations of you as their employer. Below you will find a list of the top items that meet those basic expectations. There are dozens more to consider. Those listed will give you an idea of how you should proceed.

- Employees expect that you are knowledgeable and experienced in not only your role, but in theirs as well.
- They expect clear and fair policies. Clear expectations. Procedures that are clearly outlined and modeled.
- Integrity – not only from you but from everyone within the organization.
- Clear job descriptions. Clearly define what it is you want and how it is you'd like that executed.
- Open communication.
- Opportunities for personal growth.
- Positive, consistent discipline.
- They want to feel and share in the company's success. For example, hitting a target or making a goal is not a solo operation. If management is rewarded because their employees made goal and those who actually did the work are not – that makes for an unsatisfactory response from the employees and kills morale and productivity. Look at all of the key players.

Realize that most of these needs and expectations will probably never be expressed by your employees. It is your responsibility to consider these in all of your interactions with employees. While some things cannot be helped, understanding your employees motivations and acknowledging them will work to enhance their overall job performance and allows them ownership in the process.

APPROPRIATE LEADERSHIP INTERVENTION

All interventions within an organization should be designed to help solve a problem or to achieve a very specific goal. In order to do that, you must plan the correct intervention. The starting point is to be clear about your objectives and base your decision on what it is you as the leader want to achieve. Below are some common workplace examples.

If there is a merger or an organizational restructuring, as with all other issues, you need to build the right team. To do that you need to bring people together to know what to expect from each other and how to work together in a way to bring out the best in each and every team member. Craft a team vision and define the roles of the individual team members.

To challenge existing paradigms, that team you built with the right people needs to get creative and think outside of the box. You as the employer/leader needs to provide research about changing strategic trends. Run a brainstorming session. Get the ideas flowing.

The right team can help with strategic planning when a change is necessary. They can define new roles or opportunities. Develop new strategies that will be effective after the change is implemented. Analyzing the needs of the customer or the client can be done by management and the team members.

Another appropriate intervention would be the buy-in method discussed in previous chapters. Communicate whatever that idea is to all of the employees. It is your job to get and keep them motivated and excited about contributing to the vision. Actively encourage them to contribute to the process.

If you find that the energy of the employees is lagging, an intervention strategy that you can use is to identify and deal with the root causes behind that lack of motivation or poor morale. After you've identified those look at ways to solve those problems effectively. Think like a motivational coach. Encourage change and empathize with whatever is holding them back, but don't dwell. The goal is to move on. Recognize the signs of burnout in yourself and in your employees. You may find that an appropriate intervention is a vacation – time off. That's okay. Allow that to happen. Encourage your employees to reconnect with their personal values and to create or recreate their own personal mission or vision.

IDENTIFYING JOB CHARACTERISTICS

The Job Characteristic Theory is the idea of work design. It involves having systems set in place that enrich the job experience for the employees. It is a set of principles in relation to the five core job characteristics. Those are skill variety, autonomy, task identity, task significance, and feedback. These five characteristics affect work outcomes like motivation, job satisfaction, performance, absenteeism, and turnover rates. How they affect those are through three psychological states that harken back to the needs discussed: experienced meaningfulness, knowledge of the results, and experienced responsibility.

Skill variety is the level at which the job requires various activities. If the job requires more skills and ability they are more meaningful to the employee.

Task identity is whether or not the job has a visible outcome and can the employees see that outcome. An employee will feel more involved in the process if they can see the entire process and understand how what they are doing plays into that process.

Task significance plays a major role. If the employee can see how what they do impacts lives or others internally within the organization or externally outside the organization, that enhances the meaningfulness to them.

Autonomy is the freedom to perform a job and determine the procedures in the job. This allows for ownership in the process.

Whether that means the employee takes part in the planning or the implementation or is allowed to perform the duties independently, all equate to greater personal responsibility.

Feedback deeply impacts the effectiveness of an employee's performance. Provide clear feedback in a timely manner. This increases the overall knowledge level for the employee.

EXTERNAL CONSTRAINTS

Factors outside the control of a business that inhibit or restrict the company from achieving its' goals or objectives are external constraints. Some of these are things like consumers buying habits have changed or a competitor has develop a safer or more effective product or social attitudes have changed. There are any number of factors outside of a business that can impact job performance.

Buying habits can decrease thus making productivity decrease. Warehouses become full of back stock. Employees may have their hours cut or may be laid off for a significant amount of time. Consumers may have lack of confidence in a company or product for factors beyond the employees control. All of these things can make or break productivity and decrease job ownership. Employees may want to distance themselves from the company or its products or services.

As you can see many factors contribute to enhancing job ownership and job performance. Your leadership styles as noted will play a significant role in this. Reevaluate your style and your own motivations. Discover what leadership preference works for you and, most importantly, your team. Consider factors like external constraints and look at ways that you can influence your team to press pass whatever is holding them back. Communicate and remember that employees are people. They have needs and wants like anyone else. Identify those needs. Do your part to ensure that your behavior and your leadership style takes those needs into consideration. Behaviors will change if you put in the effort to create an open environment with positive, strong leadership in mind.

CHAPTER VI

COACHING AND MANAGING EMPLOYEE PERFORMANCE

The dreaded employee review. We're all familiar with them. Once a year we sit down and talk to our employees individually and tell them what they've done well over the year and point out areas that require improvement. We, ourselves, sit in our own reviews. We listen, we nod, we agree to improve our deficiencies, but what happens next? For some, there may be initial retraining or minor tweaks to our duties. For others, after the meeting, all is forgotten. Another 365 days will roll by and we again sit down and review the same issues and the cycle continues.

As leaders, we need to take a hard look at ourselves and devise ways in which to improve that process and make a lasting impression on our employees and improve their performance. It's time to use a different, more effective, approach. Coaching is where we should be focusing our efforts. By coaching, you are giving your employees the opportunity to grow and to work harder to achieve consistent performance levels. Adhering to a schedule that promotes one yearly review per employee defeats the purpose of reviewing at all. As discussed in previous chapters, feedback must be relevant and consistent. Don't rely on solely a yearly review. It's ineffective.

You can better serve and support your employees by meeting regularly and guiding them on their paths to their personal and professional goals. Think of coaching as laying the foundation for success. You are setting the stage and allowing the employee to build upon that and produce great results. If you guide/coach them in the right way, your employees will appreciate you more and will want to improve because you motivated them and didn't belittle or berate them. Coaching is about building a working relationship, not detracting from one.

Studies have shown that hovering over your employees and managing their every move is ineffective and creates an environment of distrust. If your employees feel like you don't trust their actions, then, you are effectively telling them that you have no faith in them at all. Would you want to do your best work for a leader that had no confidence in you? That is why it is imperative that you remember that coaching as opposed to 'helicoptering' an employee is far more beneficial for all involved. You must transition from your tradition role of controlling and monitoring employees to moving into a more consultative – coaching – role. Use this style as a means for developing a partnership – allowing your employee to take ownership of their role and duties – and create a shared understanding about what the organizational needs are and exactly how to go about meeting those business needs.

Coaching has to be an ongoing process in order to be effective. This will create motivation to improve in your employees. They will have a clear understanding of how their current performance level ranks against past performance levels or future levels. It becomes in essence the litmus test for job performance. Coaching or consulting regularly will increase the likelihood of your employees being successful and feeling like their efforts have made an impact and believing in their individual contributions.

Before any coaching can begin, you, as the leader, need to identify the source of an employee's performance problem. How do you do that, you might ask? Well, you understand that every job is the responsibility of two people: the employee, who is responsible for producing an optimal result, and the manager or leader, who creates the environment where the employee works. There are key questions you can ask yourself when you are confronted with a performance problem in the workplace.

Is it a motivational problem or an ability problem? Meaning, is the employee motivated to do the job required and, if not, find out why they aren't. Or, is the job beyond the scope or ability of your employee? Look at what their duties are regarding that particular duty. Is it too much for one person to do? Is it out of their scope or reasonable knowledge base? Is there enough time allotted for the job? Are there sufficient resources readily available for your employee to use? Have your expectations and priorities been clearly defined? Is the employee's performance being recognized and rewarded? Could it be that they are burned out? Are they resentful or angry about a situation?

Any one of these questions or several running together could be the root of your problem. In most cases, these are precisely why performance has slowed or come to a halt all together. While these may not be the sum total of every conceivable problem, they are a great starting point when a problem occurs. Begin there and, if you find that they are not the core issue, ask more questions.

Excessive absenteeism could be the result of many personal problems. While it is not okay to probe, it is perfectly fine to address your concerns and brainstorm ways to ease your employee's burden. The same could be said for excessive sick leave, tardiness, having to leave work early, patterns of absenteeism. Consider their individual situations. Could it be an illness, lack of daycare, divorce, transportation issues? Perhaps your company has an employee help line or has resources via HR with dealing with issues outside of work. Recommend these tactfully and bearing in mind that these may be issues that are quite sensitive and shouldn't illicit negativity from you. Sensitivity is key. Chances are your employee understands the strain they are putting on themselves and their coworkers. Talk about ways to resolve the issues related to their job performance.

Look for behavior patterns. Know your employees. Become familiar with their lives outside of work. Doing so will help you to understand what may be going on that impacts their work. Is there a newborn at home keeping them up all night? Have they sustained an injury? Are they having financial problems? Is there a problem between coworkers?

After you have come to an agreement or solved the problem, coaching becomes crucial. What this means is that you must articulate the organization's goals in a clear, concise manner. Your employees need to understand the entire context in which they work, then, they'll have a clearer vision of how their job impacts the company. Communicating effectively will ensure that the employees remain focused and on task. Your job as the 'coach' is to establish commitment from your employees. These commitments will encourage your employees to move toward the desired goals.

Coaching is a very hands on approach that empowers employees by building their confidence and competence. You are holding them accountable for meeting set performance goals. In that respect, it's an effective tool for 'problem employees' – those deemed difficult. This managerial style is precisely the kind you need to use with difficult employees. If you are swift and just with them and provide concrete and clear expectations, you may be able to bring a resolution to a problem before it becomes a serious obstacle to the overall performance of the team or group.

Difficult employees does not necessarily refer to loud or brash employees. There are several personality types that could fall into the category of 'difficult'. They run the gamut from a particularly indecisive employee to the overly competitive employee to dramatic employees, negative employees, too social employee, and the yeller. We've seen them. We've shared space with them. We may be them. The point is they are a distraction. Their behavior needs to be controlled for the sake of every employee and in order to improve employee performance.

Just as we are all individuals, these behavior types require a specific set of actions tailored to them and their less than tolerable behavior. Let's begin with the 'yeller'. Apologizing after an outburst does not negate what they've done. Raise your intensity – intensity, not your volume. Refuse to put up with their immature behavior and, after expressing yourself, walk away. Don't allow the situation to escalate any further.

Your 'social butterfly' – assign them measurable goals. Meaning, for example, you must make a certain number of outbound calls within a reasonable time frame. Or, you must quality check 'x' number of items within 1 hours time. This will keep them on task and motivate them to perform.

The negative employee who thrives on negative attention. The key with them is giving them the right job that emphasizes their strengths. For instance, customer service advocates, quality in a call center, or any other job that would allow them to take on bureaucracy. They will thrive and do wonders for your customer service levels.

The dramatic employee – Set up boundaries for his or her behavior, letting them know that you won't tolerate in the workplace. Escort them out of meetings if you have to. Anytime they become disruptive or obstructive, immediately eject them, but give them limits. Don't allow the behavior to continue.

An overly competitive employee get him or her focused on motivating the entire team to win. Provide some sort of incentive based on the overall achievement of the team. A word of caution: this incentive should not be a paid bonus. That will destroy morale.

SUCCESSFULLY COACHING YOUR EMPLOYEES INVOLVES USING KEY SKILLS. THESE ARE:

COMMUNICATION SKILLS
- Setting a tone for discussions that fosters open and honest communication.
- Effective Listening
- Asking effective questions that solicit needed information from the employee.
- Clearly explaining your point of view in non-threatening terms.

TRAINING
- Determining employee's needed level of training.
- Demonstrating how to do important tasks/procedures.
- Observing employee practice or use what they've learned and assessing whether they are doing it properly, and if not providing additional instruction on how to do it right.

SETTING PERFORMANCE STANDARDS AND MEASURES
- Determining acceptable levels of performance for employee's tasks and responsibilities.
- Developing applicable performance measures.

PERFORMANCE ANALYSIS
- Determining if employee is performing as needed, and if not, the extent of performance gaps.
- Formulating potential solutions (additional training, behavior change, etc.)

FEEDBACK
- Providing employee with objective information on their performance.
- Delivering feedback in a non-threatening way so

employee can absorb the information and benefit from it rather than react defensively.

JOINT PROBLEM-SOLVING AND ACTION PLANNING

- Engaging the employee in determining needed corrective actions on their part to fill performance gaps.

FOLLOW-UP

- Following-up on agreed to action plans to ensure that employee is making needed corrections and following through on agreed upon commitments.

Other techniques that would be helpful when dealing with a difficult employee include adjusting to their personality. When having a discussion with them, ensure you do so in a way that fits their personality and their comfort level. Don't be confrontational, but do remain firm. Some may prefer private one-on-one conversations. Others may demand a discussion in the middle of the work area. Things will smooth over much easier if you discuss matters where they are comfortable if at all possible. Never get into a shouting match. Never have private discussions in front of visitors or customers. Remain calm and direct.

Document, document, document. This a must on each and every occasion. There must be a record of every conversation, transgression, negotiation, disciplinary action, etc. Document in detail their mistakes and their behavior. If allowed per company policy, keep a personal log in addition to the one filed with HR or any other procedure pertinent. All documentation that goes into their employee file must be signed by them. If they refuse, that must be noted and addressed. You will save yourself and them a lot of unforeseen problems by documenting everything.

Follow proper disciplinary procedures. As much as you may want to, you cannot simply fire someone because they irritate you. There are steps and procedures in place. Utilize them. Know your policies and follow them. Ensure that each of your employees has a clear understanding of the policies and procedures.

Ask the right questions. As mentioned earlier, is this job not a good fit for them? Could their talents be utilized in other positions or other departments? Don't transfer a problem for the sake of getting rid of them. Make sure that the move is in their best interest not your own.

Bring someone else in to talk to them. The situation may have escalated beyond repair. Allow someone else to step in and diffuse the situation or be a mediator if necessary. Just the simple act of having someone neutral hear them out may lessen the burden for all involved.

Finally, consider that they may be bored or burned out. Offer them a challenge. Give them different duties, difficult tasks, or a change of scenery. It may be a matter of not being satisfied by what they are doing anymore. You might be surprised to see a positive change because you thought outside of the box.

Know that coaching and managing employees doesn't have to be a daunting task. It doesn't require extensive research or obtaining a degree in human relations. With a few simple techniques, you can create an environment where employees thrive and performance levels increase exponentially and, most importantly, have happy, productive employees that enjoy their jobs and know and understand their duties and know their limitations.

TRUE OR FALSE QUIZ

Coaching is using specific skills to train your employees to perform their required duties.

True   False

Standing guard over your employees builds an effective working relationship.

True   False

Trust is not needed in the work environment.

True   False

Employees opinions don't matter.

True   False

Use shouting matches to discipline employees.

True   False

Transfer any employee who challenges you.

True   False

Take the time to get to know your employees and become familiar with their outside responsibilities.

True   False

Abrasive employees make for good motivators.

True   False

VERBAL WARNING FORM

Date:_____

Overview:

Employee:

Brief Overview (To be completed by employee

_____

_____

_____

_____

Is This The First Time Verbal Counseling Has Been Conducted:

Yes   No

If No, Was The Previous Verbal Counseling For The Same Issue

Yes   No

If Yes, Is Documentation Of Previous Communication Attached

Yes   No

Summary Of Communication With Employee

Employee Is Expected To Do The Following
What Others Will Do To Support This
Additional Training Or Development
Follow Up Communication With Employee
Supervisor's Signature

CORRECTIVE ACTION PROCESS

Oral warning - An oral warning is a discussion between the supervisor and the employee which identifies the problem issue and communicates a clear expectation that changes must be forthcoming or more a more serious disciplinary step will follow. The next step does not automatically follow, but in many cases, an oral warning that is not heeded results in the next step.

Written warning - A written warning is a formal document created by the supervisor and given to the employee. The written warning is used when previous efforts to correct the deficient performance or behavior has failed. Depending upon the circumstances, a problem may be sufficiently severe such that a supervisors decides to move directly to a written warning. Written warnings are signed by the employee and supervisor. If witnesses are present, they too sign the warning. A copy of the warning is sent to Human Resources where it is placed in the employees personnel file.

Suspension, demotion or dismissal - These three actions represent the most serious steps in the disciplinary process because they result in serious job altering consequences for the employee. Typically, they would be implemented only after the other efforts have been unsuccessful.

A GUIDE TO EMPLOYEE COUNSELING:

Counseling

Counseling is similar to coaching in that it shares the same goal, improving performance and/or stopping inappropriate workplace behaviors. With counseling, however, the meeting between the supervisor and the employee takes on a different feel. In such meetings the supervisor attempts to understand and identify the issues contributing to the performance or behavioral problem. Accordingly, in a counseling meeting, the supervisor is focused on listening, verifying their understanding of the problem and engaging in problem-solving with the employee. Like the coaching transaction, the supervisor and the employee leave the counseling meeting with a corrective plan in mind. Counseling is letting the employee know that the supervisor takes the issue seriously and wants to help them get past it. At the same time, the message is clear from the supervisor--the employee's performance must improve, behaviors must change or more serious steps will have to be taken.

SIX STEPS TO COACHING

1. Relationship
2. Aspiration
3. Assessment
4. Goal Setting
5. Action Planning and Review
6. Achievement Recognition

Site: *http://coachcampus.com/coach-portfolios/coaching-models/ harish-devarajanl-raaga/*

CHAPTER VII

MANAGING AND RESOLVING CONFLICT

LEARNING TO IDENTIFY conflicts and be a proactive leader will make for a better working experience for everyone within your organization. Identifying potential issues doesn't happen naturally for most of us, unless we've studied people and their motivations thoroughly in the past, we are going to fail miserably at this task. There are simple steps to take that will help you to identify small issues before they become too large to handle.

Oftentimes, management will overlook vital components because their eye is on the big picture. They develop this sort of tunnel vision and only monitor how close they are to a particular goal. While this is fine, it neglects an area that could cause a ripple effect throughout the entire company. It'd be easy to say, "Everything looks fine. The team is productive." However, is there potential for more productivity? Are your team members happy? Is there anything that is preventing them from doing anything seamlessly?

While thinking about those aspects may seem counter-intuitive to the process, they are the very items you must take into consideration. What seems trivial could in fact be a point of contention between staff members. Explore minor issues or the potential for minor issues.

You may be asking how these apply when we are speaking about identifying conflict within a workplace. The answer is that all matters apply whether they are large or small. Conflicts can arise for various reasons and in the unlikeliest of situations. There is a theory, identified by psychologists Art Bell and Brett Hart (2000 and 2002), that states that conflicts can be classified into eight distinct causes. They are as follows:

1. **Conflicting resources**
2. **Conflicting styles**
3. **Conflicting perceptions**
4. **Conflicting goals**
5. **Conflicting pressures**
6. **Conflicting roles**
7. **Different personal values**
8. **Unpredictable policies**

Conflicting Resources is exactly what it says it is. If you or your team members do not have all of the resources necessary to fulfill their job requirements, conflict will arise. This has a simple solution provided that you have all the resources and tools available to you or can gain access to wherever those supplies may be or where they are ordered from and under whose authority. Circumvent any conflict by ensuring that every member of the team has exactly what they need to get their job done.

You may be asking what to do when budget cuts loom or a company is the middle of a takeover or cash strapped. This is where strong communication skills come in. The employees need to know what is happening and together you must brainstorm other ways to get the same job done. While doing so can be stressful, it is not impossible, by any means. Open discussions will help employees to vent their frustrations, then, ideas can be brainstormed to find a working solution. As a group prioritize what needs to be done with what you have and put a new system in place to accomplish tasks. Respect the needs of your employees. Sometimes there is no viable solution. That needs to be communicated to resolve any underlying tension.

Conflicting Styles refers to how one person works versus another. If those two styles don't blend seamlessly, conflict could occur. For instance, if one member of your team works exceptionally fast and another is slow and steady, they could clash if placed on the same team or given the task of completing a task together. Having them work side-by-side will cause undue stress for both of them. Know your employees work personalities. Notice how they work. Become familiar with their style and choose accordingly when assigning tasks or building a team.

While this may not always be information you are privy to, especially when faced with new staff members, it is your responsibility to monitor how your employees work and react accordingly. If you feel that two styles may not blend well together, do what it takes to make sure you don't add pressure to the situation. Work is not the place for encouraging one to work like the other if that style isn't their own. Avoid making them feel like they have to compete with a team member. If, individually, what they do works, don't force an unnecessary change.

Conflicting Perceptions can wreak havoc on the workplace. We all have our own ideas and beliefs. What you may see as red, another may see as blue. Our perceptions stem from upbringing, culture, personality, and environment. When perceptions clash a sort of turf war begins. Recognizing that before it escalates will save everyone a world of trouble. Make efforts to eliminate any conflict before it happens. Communicate openly with your team members to ensure everyone is on the same page. Don't get caught in a game of words. Don't tell one group one thing and another something different. Even if those two conversations essentially say the same thing, they can be perceived as different ideas entirely. Use the same speech for both groups. Hit the same targets. Information breeds power and having the same information will lessen the likelihood of conflicting perceptions.

Conflicting Goals are another sources of workplace conflict. This applies to management as well. Make sure everyone is on the same page. One manager may tell the team to concentrate on one step while another has already asked that another step be concentrated on. This causes confusion and is a breeding ground for workplace strife.

When you set goals with your team, your job is to make sure that Goal A and Goal B don't conflict with one another. Are you perhaps putting the cart before the horse? This is where prioritizing which tasks to need to be done and how they need to be done becomes important. Don't send your team out to complete a job without telling them the how, what, where, why, and when. Everyone needs a clear goal and everyone needs to be on board with that goal.

Conflicting Pressures – Do your employees have too many tasks assigned to them? Are the deadlines conflicting or adding to much pressure to their daily lives? When delegating jobs have a realistic time line in mind. Don't expect too much too soon and don't delegate everything to one person or one group.

This, like conflicting goals, puts undue pressure on people and can cause production to slow down or to be lacking. Your goal should be quality work in a timely fashion. Reevaluate time lines for the tasks you've assigned and ask yourself if they seem realistic.

Conflicting Roles can occur when you as the manager do not make it clear who is to do what and when. If, for instance, you enlist help from a couple of team members to work on a task with other team members – perhaps one who is a supervisor – their role and duties can become confusing. In some instances, a little more control or a little less control while doing a task makes it difficult to see where exactly they stand. Are they now in charge? Could they, perhaps, give orders or delegate tasks now that they've been allowed to work side-by-side with a supervisor? Again, communicating exactly what their task is and what their parameters are will ease this process for everyone and won't muddy the waters for the group as a whole.

Different Personal Values – Are you asking someone to do something that may go against their personal or ethical standards? If that's the case, you have created a situation where different personal values become a source of contention. To avoid this, the idea is simple, practice ethical leadership. While it may be easier to skim over the rules or regulations or to cheat a little here and there – for the sake of everyone involved – follow the guidelines that have been set in place. They won't steer you wrong and they won't undermine your authority. Your team members will respect you for honoring codes and for respecting their moral compass.

Unpredictable Policies are inevitable in the workplace. Policies and procedures are updated, eliminated, or what have you all the time. These changes implemented without communication to every staff member is a failure. Confusion will cause conflict. Communicate what the changes are, how they will affect everyone, when they will go into effect, and thoroughly communicate how those changes will be rolled out. Employees will want to know why. Have an honest answer for them. You will get better responses when you give an honest answer to sometimes tough questions. Explain what you know and stay within your scope.

IDENTIFYING CONFLICTS QUIZ

Circle the best option.

Upper management has just advised that the office supply budget be cut in your customer service department. They advise that costs be cut by 1/3 of your annual budget. You've brainstormed ways in which you could reduce costs in your department. Currently ball point

pens are $5.00 per package of 100. Every employee has access to pens as needed. Monthly you purchase 3 packages. These are the pens the staff has indicated that they like to use. You notice that a package of pencils costs $3.00 for 200 pencils. You buy 3 packages of pencils for the following month, believing this is the best solution and remove all of the existing pens from your department and issue pencils for everyone. How would you communicate this to your employees?

A. Send an email stating that pens are no longer allowed.
B. Say nothing and hope the staff doesn't notice.
C. Meet with your employees before making a decision and discuss options.

Your department is one week shy of a vital deadline. You've had one trusted employee working on it. Although his method is slow, he is efficient. With this deadline looming, you worry that this special project won't be completed in time. Another employee works very fast and is eager to help. Asking the faster employee to pitch in would seem like the logical choice, so you quickly fill them in on the details and set them off to work side-by-side by the other employee who has spent the last 3 weeks working on this project alone. What do you think the result of this decision will be on this employee?

A. They will be glad to have the help.
B. They will resent you for calling in reinforcements.
C. The slower employee will learn to work twice as fast.

WHICH OF THESE WOULD BE AN EXAMPLE OF CONFLICTING GOALS?

A. Delegating new tasks to a seasoned employee.
B. A manager wants you to skew the results of a test.
C. One of your supervisors has given the employees two hours to complete a task before she leaves for the day. The evening supervisor comes in and tells you to save the task for the following day.

AVOID DESTRUCTIVE COMMUNICATION, IDENTIFY CAUSES

Think of communication as a road map. You make choices with every word that comes out of your mouth. This is true for everyone, no matter what the situation. The key is to know which road you'll take. Look at how you speak or express feelings when you're facing a difficult situation or becoming upset. Take note of how others do that as well. For most of us, we tend to lean toward a side that may not be the best course for us. We are reacting without thinking. That is like taking the wrong road and ending up going in circles.

Talking ourselves into circles leaves us unsatisfied and unable to resolve conflicts. We become upset and begin to nitpick at minor differences. Having the ability to recognize these communication failures in our own lives, will allow us to see some of the same patterns in others. Doing so gives us just enough information to learn how to avoid destructive communication and to identify the underlying causes of it.

As discussed, minor issues or what we deem as minor issues could be troubling someone in the office. We don't need to know about their personal lives, if that's where the problem stems, but we do need to be armed with the tools to help us recognize that something is not right. Recognizing it is not solving it. More in depth analysis needs to be made without crossing a line.

We aren't counselors or therapists. We are coworkers regardless of your position or status. If you work for the same organization, you are a coworker. On the same token, your superiority doesn't negate common rules of behavior. All parties near and far must be treated with respect. That respect cannot simply be implied, but must be in use at all times.

How can we identify destructive communication? The answer is in various ways. Look at the clues around you. Watch the body language. Listen to tones. Is the language harsh or demeaning? Are jokes off-color or hurtful? Has the rumor mill begun amongst staff? While these are not the only indicators of a communication breakdown, they are clear signs that something has gone awry. It doesn't take a genius to see when things are getting bad. Follow your gut. Speak to your people. Hear their concerns. Nip whatever potential problem there is in the bud. You know your people.

While we've spoken about body language previously, it bears repeating. Understand non-verbal communication. On the following page, we have provided a worksheet to refresh your memory.

NON-VERBAL COMMUNICATION/BODY LANGUAGE

1. Eye movements – winking, blinking, twitching
2. Hand movements – waving, clapping, clasping
3. Head movements – nodding, shaking
4. Appearance – untidiness
5. Posture – slouching
6. Ways of talking – pauses, stress on words
7. Sounds – laughing, crying
8. Closeness – invading someone's space
9. Body Contact – shaking hands
10. Facial Expression – frowning, eyebrow furrowing

Body Language	Possible Meaning
Avoiding Eye Contact	Lying, Not Interested, Not telling the whole truth
Serious Eye Contact	Trying to intimidate, showing anger
Touching the face/fidgeting	Nervousness, Lack of Confidence, Submission
Nodding	Agreeing, Willing to compromise
Shaking the head/turning away	Frustrated, In Disbelief, Disagreeing with a point

WHAT MAKES AN IMPRESSION?

How you speak = 38%
Your words = 7%
Your Body Language = 55%

COMMUNICATION SKILLS BROKEN DOWN

Oral

Presentation
Audience Awareness
Critical Listening
Body Language

Written

Academic Writing
Revision and Editing
Critical Reading
Presentation of Data

Non-Verbal

Audience Awareness
Personal Presentation
Body Language

ASSESS PERSONAL STRENGTHS AND DEVELOPMENTAL NEEDS IN DETERMINING THE BEST APPROACH TO MANAGING CONFLICT

In order to manage conflict within the workplace we must know where our strengths and weaknesses lie in terms of conflict management. Just like we ask potential employees to answer specific questions during an interview related to that topic, we can ask ourselves those same questions. How do we handle conflict when it arises? What have we done in the past? What was the best approach? Which approach didn't work? Below we will look at some answers to those very questions and see where we stand as leaders.

CONFLICT RESOLUTION QUESTIONS

Discuss a time when you and a reporting employee disagreed about a direction, how you handled a situation, a performance review, or suggestions for improvement. How did you handle the disagreement?

When you've witnessed employees who were in conflict and

disagreed with each other on important issues, what was your preferred approach for helping the employee resolve the conflict?

Think of a time when you worked with a coworker who would seem to agree with the direction decided by a group. But, for weeks or months later, the coworker continued to raise objections to the decisions made by the group. How did you address this situation with your coworker? If you didn't discuss it, what were you thinking about when you decided not to confront the ongoing problem?

How comfortable are you, in general, with dealing with differences of opinion and disagreements? Can you provide a work-related example that illustrates your comfort level?

The leader of a team on which you participate consistently talks more than all of the members of the group. Consequently, his views largely direct the actions of the team. He is smart, wants participation, wants the other members to step up, but no one practices the professional courage necessary to make the team successful. What would you do in this situation?

When you think about your experience with disagreement and conflict resolution, how would you rate your skills in handling differences of opinion? Give an example.

While there is no 'best' approach to conflict resolution, there are techniques that can ease tensions, if utilized correctly. We've examined many before, but we'll offer a few more to use in your arsenal against conflicts within the workplace.

Listen, Then Speak – Sometimes the easiest thing you can do is to simply listen. That in itself may diffuse the entire situation. This, regardless of the situation, should be your first line of defense. People want to be heard, not judged.

Gather the Group – As the leader, you will need to bring all sides/ parties together. Arrange a meeting. Discuss the issues. Give everyone a chance to speak. This is the best opportunity to hear all sides of the problem and to be able to formulate a plan to resolve the issues. If expedited correctly, the solution should satisfy all parties. There will be no one true winner, but you can come to a consensus.

Be Impartial – Don't take sides! In a leadership position, you shouldn't favor one opinion or one side over another. Assess the problem from all sides and leave your personal feelings out of the equation.

Do Not Postpone Conflict Resolution – Address all problems immediately before they escalate out of control. This is the most effective conflict resolution and will make the employees feel that their issues are important to you too.

Promote Teamwork – Encourage your team to work together. Keep them working toward the same goal. Remind them of other times when they came together and succeeded at a task.

Broadcast Praise – Encourage employees with positive words and thanks. Spread the word about how great they are doing. Model positive behavior and encourage others to follow the successes of others. Praise will spread like a virus and others will seek it out and, in turn, that may quell any squabbles.

Conflict resolution is the art of negotiation. You are not there to add fuel to the fire or to complicate matters. Your goal is to not leave room for conflict. Beat it to the punch. Be proactive in your approach. Think beyond the big picture and look at the every moment nuances. Follow the cues of those working for and with you. Understand their concerns. Their concerns should be your concerns. That doesn't mean that you should choose sides or input your own opinion to contradict the ones already up for debate. You should be seeking a solution that will meet everyone's needs as long as they are in line with the values of the company. Don't go out of your way to change a policy because one of the employees is bullying others or you for a change. Do what works best so as not to halt production. You are dealing with individuals. Treat them as such.

CHAPTER VIII

PROBLEM-SOLVING AND DECISION-MAKING

IN EVERY STAGE OF LIFE WE ARE TASKED with having to solve problems. This is a given. There's no way around it – no way that would make sense in any aspect of our lives. We are often left with more questions than answers in these situations. So, you need to have a plan. A strategy must be set in place. There's simply no avoiding it.

Instead of becoming overwhelmed by a mountain of questions, begin by asking the right question: What's the most efficient way to get this done? Figuring that out will solve a host of other issues for you. Why take more steps than necessary? That can only lead to confusion and frustration. Neither of either of these states is where you want to find yourself at work.

As human beings we often have our go-to practices. One would be: wishing the problem away causes more problems in the long run. Believing that your initial answer has to be the best answer can cause undue stress. There is no hitting the ball out of the park on the first try strategy involved. Lastly, deflecting blame or responsibility to someone else. We do this all the time to avoid having to deal with a problem.

Remember two key facts about any problem in life and, for our purposes, within the workplace. Problems occur all the time. Often they happen through no fault of our own and cannot be prevented. Secondly, they are opportunities for growth or change. The end result of most problems is having a system that is improved to prevent issues in the future.

No matter the problem, there is an efficient way to work toward a solution. Mind you, not all problems will be resolved in the manner that we hope for, but every resolution begins with building a road that includes steps to making progress.

First, you must identify what exactly the problem is. Be clear about it. Is it the process as a whole or is one part of the process or one part of the equation infecting other components? Remember, we are all human. What you see as a problem may not seem like such a big deal to someone else. Get other eyes on the problem, so to speak. Have an objective person take a look at the situation and give you feedback about it. Their opinion may be vastly different from your own.

Next, after you've had other opinions and input from interested parties, clearly state what the real issue is. It may be larger than you initially believed or it may be far less of a concern than you initially thought.

Keep everyone's best interest in mind. Understand their thoughts and opinions. This is crucial to the process because missing something could mean altering the results. Detach yourself personally from the situation. Whatever happened didn't occur just to thwart your efforts. The problem isn't about you. Take the time to listen to those around you. Set aside any differences and come to a consensus as to how to move forward. The best solution, you'll find, stems from satisfying everyone's needs.

Do some brainstorming, if there's time. Allow room to let ideas and solutions flow. Take the time to evaluate possible solutions or to combine certain elements of varied solutions.

Get buy-in on solutions in writing. Document what the agreed solution is. Make your case, then, once some form of agreement is made, document it and make the same information available for everyone that will be affected and for all senior management members. Writing these matters down will help everyone to think clearly and to work toward the same goal without having to stop and guess what the next step should be. It'll be right there in front of them to review and self-check.

If there is a possible kink in the solution that's being proposed, have a contingency plan that everyone has agreed on. Conditions could change and that needs to be taken into account in the beginning. Again, document the contingency plans and roll them out as agreed. Have someone responsible for monitoring compliance and follow-through. How will you know if the plan worked if you haven't evaluated it? Have a time frame in mind for your solution. Say, 'If after 30 days, the system/task/issue hasn't been positively impacted, we'll try _____'. That leaves your options open and prevents the same full scale problem from happening again.

Again, there are no hard and fast rules to problem-solving, only techniques. The above is one example. We will explore different examples as we proceed. Depending on the kind of problem you may be having, the steps can vary widely. Use what suits the situation best for you and your organization.

Simple Problem-Solving Techniques

- Ask yourself, "What's the most efficient way to solve this problem?"
- Seek assistance. Ask for the opinions of others. Have someone else look at the problem and respect their point of view.
- Remove yourself from the problem. It's not about you. This is for the good of everyone around you.
- Identify the problem clearly. Pick it apart and take note of which part is failing.

- Keep everyone's best interest in mind. Again, this problem and/or solution is not about you.
- Do some brainstorming with your team.
- Take the time to evaluate all possible solutions.
- Document what the agreed solution is – every point. Make that information available for all parties involved and members of upper management. Don't leave people in the dark. That makes for bad business.
- Have a contingency plan. No solution is set in stone. Systems fail. People fail. Be prepared for whatever may come next.
- Give the solution a time line. Finding a solution isn't the end of the road. Remaining free of that particular problem in the long run is what justifies a solution. Make your time line realistic. This is not fix it and forget it.

lgorithms are often discussed and evaluated. While many people believe they have a good grasp of algorithms, there is a large percentage of people for whom it makes no sense. How they apply to problem-solving may help people to understand them better.

An algorithm is a step-by-step procedure that will always produce a correct solution. Often you'll find algorithms used in mathematical equations. For instance, a mathematical formula is an algorithm. We've seen them. We've used formulas in school. But, while an algorithm guarantees an accurate answer, it's not always the best approach to problem-solving. Why do I tell you this? The answer is because when a problem occurs, those of us that think this way, approach problems from this standpoint and often end up creating a bigger problem for ourselves. For example, if you were trying to figure out all the possible number combinations for a lock system using an algorithm, it would take a very long time.

This section is designed to show you that while algorithms may be appropriate in some situations, they're often not appropriate in the workplace.

If you are mathematically inclined, there is a math strategy that may apply to some problems – heuristics. Fancy word, but what does it mean? Those who are mathematically inclined will know. For the rest of us, the answer is – a heuristic is a mental rule-of-thumb strategy that may or may not work in certain situations. Unlike algorithms, heuristics do not always guarantee a correct solution. However, using this problem-solving strategy does allow people to simplify complex problems and reduce the total number of possible solutions to a more manageable set.

Trial-and-Error is another approach to problem-solving. A trial-and-error approach to problem-solving involves trying a number of different solutions and ruling out those that do not work. This approach can be a good option if you have a very limited number of options at your disposal. If there are many different choices, you're better off narrowing down the possible options using another problem-solving technique before attempting trial-and-error.

In some cases, the solution to a problem can appear as a sudden **insight**. Insight can occur because you realize that the problem is actually similar to something that you have dealt with in the past, but in most cases the underlying mental processes that lead to insight happen outside of awareness.

Of course, problem-solving is not a flawless process. There are a number of different obstacles that can interfere with our ability to solve a problem quickly and efficiently. Below, we will discuss some of those mental obstacles.

Functional Fixedness is a term that refers to the tendency to view problems only in their customary manner. Functional fixedness prevents people from fully seeing all of the different options that might be available to find a solution.

Using **irrelevant and misleading information**. When you are trying to solve a problem, it's important to distinguish between information that is relevant to the issue and irrelevant data that can lead to faulty solutions. When a problem is very complex, the easier it becomes to focus on misleading or irrelevant information.

When dealing with a problem, people often make assumptions about the constraints and obstacles that prevent certain solutions.

Another common problem-solving obstacle is known as a mental set, which is the tendency people have to only use solutions that have worked in the past rather than looking for alternative ideas. A mental set can often work as a heuristic, making it a useful problem-solving tool. However, mental sets can also lead to inflexibility, making it more difficult to find effective solutions.

Problem-solving Techniques To Improve Creativity

- **Newspaper Headline** – Try writing your problem as if it were a headline in a newspaper. You can write it as if the problem still exists, or as if the problem were already solved. Try Tabloid headlines for even more creative ideas.

- **Future Party** – Imagine it's one year from today; what did you solve in the last year? How is the world different based on the solution? What were the steps you took to solve the problem?

- **40-20-10-5** – Explain your problem in up to 40 words. Then, cut it down to 20 words; then to 10; then finally to only five words. These five words are the root of your problem and likely the root of your solution as well.

- **Explain Life I'm Five** – Explain your problem as if you were talking to a five year old kid. Use basic language and simple metaphors if necessary.

- **Ad Game** – Have people mill about the room. When someone offers up an idea, everyone emphatically says "Yes!" and then the group continues to generate ideas, often building off the last idea that was offered.

- **Craziest Idea First** – Hold a contest to get the craziest idea out first. Encourage everyone to think of the absolute craziest possible solutions to the problem. After you have a long list, go back through and see which ones may not be all that crazy.

- **What Would X Do** – Pretend you're someone famous (or someone you admire) and ask yourself how they would solve the problem, what options would they consider?

- **10x10x10 Matrix** – Generate a list of 10 ideas for solving the problem. Pick one of those ideas and generate 10 variations of that idea. Pick one idea from the new list and generate 10 more variations.

- **Decide on a Solution** – Problem-solving activities that help narrow your list of possible solutions down to the best solution.

- **Futures Wheel** – Pick a possible solution and write it in the center of a piece of paper. List possible direct results/consequences of the solution around the center idea. List possible indirect results/consequences based on the direct results/consequences.

- **Thiagi's 35** – Use a point system to determine the preferred solution among your team, turning a possibly subjective discussion into an objective group decision.

- **Idea Trial** – When you can't get agreement on which solution to choose, have the proponents of each idea represent them in 'court'. Go through opening arguments, call witnesses and allow closing statements. Have the project board choose the winner.

- **Coin-Flip** – When deciding between two equally good solutions, flip a coin. When the coin is in the air, take note of what you secretly hope the result is and go with that (if you really can't decide between the two, then go with the actual result of the coin-flip).

- **End in Mind** – To create your plan, start with the end in mind and work backwards. Establish key milestones and dates in reverse order, starting with the end-of-project celebration and ending with today.

- **Idea Mock-ups** – Create a mock-up of the solution. You can create physical mock-up using various supplies in your office or a virtual mock-up using images from around the web.

- **Gamification** – Turn the completion of your project into a game. Establish rules for how you earn points, create badges to celebrate milestones and track game progress.

- **Be a Character** – Add some fun to your work by executing your plan as if you were a fictional character. Think about how they would operate and get into character.

- **Apply the McLuhan Tetrad of Questions** – Answer McLuhan's tetrad of questions in context of your solution: 1) What does your solution enhance? 2) What does it make obsolete? 3) What does it bring back that was once obsolete? And 4) What does it flip into when taken to the extreme?

- **Word on the Street** – Conduct word-on-the-street type interviews with members of your team, asking them how they felt about the project and the solution.

- **Stop-Start-Continue** – Review the way you completed your project and pick activities you should stop (things you did on this project that you don't think are necessary for future projects), start (things you didn't do on this project but that you should do on future projects) and continue (things you did on the project that you should do on future projects).

- **Find the Funny** – Write a monologue or stand-up set that covers some of the funny moments or ideas from the project. Share it with your team.

Employees rely on you to make transitions smooth. You can ensure a smooth transition by encouraging your team to buy-in to the change.

While this has been discussed previously in terms of establishing buy-in for change, the same techniques can be applied to problem-solving. After a viable solution has been implemented, you will want to get your team members on board.

Your job will involve touting the benefits of this change because that's exactly what it is – a different way of doing things. Let them hear and see you utilizing the new techniques or strategies. Don't begrudge the process or the problem that caused the change. Explain at great length how this new process or technique will benefit everyone involved. Remember, again, solving problems bears everyone in mind. That's how business works. No project is truly a solo project.

Creative Problem-solving Test

Answer 1 – completely true 2 – mostly true 3 – somewhat true 4 – mostly false 5 – completely false

- The fear of making a mistake effects many of the decisions I make.
- When faced with a problem, I try to look at it from different angles in order to come up with the best solution.
- I have complete faith in my capabilities and skills.
- If I could, I'd prefer to let other people make difficult decisions for me.
- Change in general makes me uneasy.
- Making snap decisions makes me uncomfortable.
- When others get stuck, I am able to think of new solutions to problems.
- I don't think it's necessary to come up with new solutions to a problem if the one I've used in the past was successful.
- I believe that no matter what life throws at me, I'll be able to handle it.
- Asking for other people's ideas about how to solve a problem is a sign of a lack of skill on my part.
- Once I've found a solution that I believe will work, I see no point in coming up with more.
- I like learning new things.
- I get really nervous when I have to make an important decision.
- I'm the type of person who thinks outside the box.

- When faced with a difficult problem I tend to get discouraged easily.
- I'm not sure if I've done a good job unless someone else points it out.
- After I've made a decision, I find myself wishing I had chosen differently.
- I enjoy trying new things.
- Your company needs to come up with a new ad campaign to sell your latest product and your superior chooses you as project manager. During a brainstorming meeting, your youngest team member – new hire fresh out of school – comes up with an idea that, although sounds crazy, could end up being really successful. Unfortunately, the veterans on your team who've had years of experience in marketing don't seem to be too enthusiastic about it. You yourself don't seem to be completely sold on it either, and actually had something completely different in mind. However, this new ad campaign is geared towards a younger audience – just about the same ages as the newest employee – and he/she really seems to be on top of what's hot these days. What do you do? a) thank him/her for their idea, but turn it down. I'd rather go with a plan that has proven to be successful. b) give him/her a chance c) run it through the other members of the team and weigh the pros and cons d) decide to give it a try and not worry about the resistance of the others
- Your work team has recently encountered a problem similar to one you confronted in the past with another company. The solution you came up with at your previous job ended up working out really well. However, while brainstorming together with your current team, they end up coming up with a completely different solution, one that you've never thought of before – and aren't sure will work. How do you react? a) insist they use the old solution b) ask the team members to consider the way you know worked in the past for you c) accept that there may be more than one way to solve the problem d) feel good about the new idea and look forward to positive results

Creative problem-solving is a method of using imagination along with cognitive techniques, such as analogies, associations and other mechanisms, to help produce insights into problems which might not otherwise be obtained through conventional, traditional methods.

Your answers may vary widely, but know that in general if your answers remain one way or another, that means that you tend to skew all problem-solving in that way. Are you in the middle? Are you highly skewed one way or the other?

CHAPTER IX

CHANGE MANAGEMENT

IT'S INEVITABLE THAT CHANGE WILL BE RESISTED. What can management do to plan and implement a change program more effectively? While there are no hard and fast ways to implement change, there are strategies that will make the transition easier for everyone involved.

First, you must identify the changes that are absolutely required. Then, you must determine the major issues that need to be addressed. Identifying and assessing the key stakeholders will save a lot of time and stress. Who is involved? Who will it affect? You'll also need to win the support of those key individuals and be able to identify the obstacles. Determine the degree of risk and the cost of change before attempting to implement change. Understand why change will be resisted and how it can be managed and, then, you'll know how to circumvent any potential issues.

As in most cases, people are the key factor in overcoming resistance to change. The successful implementation of new working methods and practices or integrating new businesses into a group is dependent upon the willing and effective co-operation of employees and management. Many initiatives and programs fail because they are derailed by the people factor.

A key part of successful change is building and communicating the reasons and the vision for change. Employees need to be clear about what a change involves and how they are involved in it:

- What is involved?
- What are the proposed changes?
- What is the timescale?
- Why should we do it?
- What will the major effects be?

Various techniques can be adopted which help ease a change process, including:

- Cross-functional teams
- Stronger internal communication
- Negotiation
- Action planning
- Appointing change events or champions of change
- And a certain amount of compulsion manipulation and coercion

The trick is to help employees and managers accept change more easily: top management need to:

- Act decisively – demonstrate momentum
- Consider how they will be affected
- Involve them in the change
- Consult and inform frequently
- Be firm but flexible
- Monitor the change

Change Management aims to ensure that programs, systems, personnel and management are sufficiently prepared for change so they can operate to a satisfactory level of performance until the transition has been fully adopted and implemented.

Transition and change is not the same thing. Change is situational. Transitional is psychological. These are two different processes and each must be managed vigilantly in order for the desired modification to the system or program to be successful. Even with well designed and detailed plans put in place, the change can easily fail if the transition phase is ignored. It is imperative to manage people through the transitions that take place when change is introduced. Transitions travel through three distinct phases; The Ending, The Neutral Zone, and the New Beginning.

The Ending is a period of letting go of the old way. Often there is an emotional tie, a sense of identify and a feeling of competence that is being removed from the current program or system.

The Neutral Zone is an in between time, when the old way is gone but the new isn't fully operational. It is also a period when the workforce may feel least confident or comfortable in their positions. What used to be second nature and something they were good at is now creating feelings of inadequacy and doubt.

The New Beginning is when people develop the new identify, are competent again at their job and have made it through the change successfully with a new sense of purpose. This is the phase where the implemented change really begins to work.

If the transition isn't carefully planned and people aren't carefully managed through each phase, the change could take twice as long to implement or it may fail all together. Often managers rush through the transition periods or ignore them all together. Managers who have been a part of the change development and planning process are often at the New Beginning phase before the affected workforce even makes it into The Ending; they fail to recognize the emotional impact because they no longer feel the loss themselves.

In order to implement effective change, you will need a

structured plan. Below is an example of an effective plan that you may want to consider.

Change Management Policy and Objectives

- Change Policy
- Objectives of the Change Management Plan

Data Collection and Planning

- Identification of the Problem
- Management Commitment and Responsibilities
- Change Management Accountabilities
- Appointment of key personnel to the project
- Gap Analysis
- Incorporate a communication plan
- Implement Documentation Process

Change Risk Management Processes

- Define the scope and scale of the operational problem
- Development of Risk Assessment
- Identification of a benefit vs. cost process

Change Implementation Process

- Measurement of Success

Change Management Promotion Process

- Change Management Communication processes
- Training in preparation for the change implementation

Safety Assurance Processes

- Monitoring of change activities and methods
- Data gathering throughout the change implementation and transition

- Continuous improvement to the change management plan

Transition Management

- Assessing Transition Readiness
- Planning for the transition
- Developing a Transition Monitoring Team
- The Leaders Role in Times of Transition

Change Management Documentation

- Change policy and objectives
- Change processes and procedures
- Accountabilities, responsibilities and authorities
- Mechanism for ongoing involvement of management, implementation teams and program personnel
- Change training programs, training requirements and attendance records
- Change outputs of findings from implementation of change and transition processes

The change process is a very visible means of expressing commitment by leadership and encouraging participation throughout an organization. It is the primary channel of setting the tone for communication throughout the process and establishes support by providing sufficient resources to accomplish necessary objectives. The policy is the initial method of communication from leadership for change to the system or program. It identifies why change management is important, what methods and processes the organization intends to use to achieve the desired outcomes and how these methods and processes will be employed into operations.

When setting objectives for the change management plan they must be specific, measurable realistic and agreed with by those who have to deliver them. Ensure the objectives are approved by the accountable senior manager. Set short and long-term objectives that will continued to direct the change management process through the transition period. Set indicators and targets the will keep the process on track to achieve the objectives. Communicate the objectives to foster a common understanding of what the change management process is set to achieve.

Problems are what normally lead to a change. When a problem is recognized at a level where it requires consideration for change implementation, begin a preliminary information gathering and documentation process. It is important to recognize which program or systems to which the change management process pertains as well as other programs or systems that may be impacted. The problem should be sufficiently identified and preliminary actions recorded.

1. What is the problem, event or catalyst that is creating a decision leading toward this change?
2. What program or system does the problem and eventual change apply to?
3. Collect information about the problem from those closest to it.
4. Engage people in the problem-solving process.

- Gain peoples investment in the process which will in turn gain their interest in the outcome.
- Work to acquire the influence of the most effective and respected people within that system or program.
- Try to understand what interests are currently in place that people might try to protect when facing transitions caused by this change.

5. Communicate the problem throughout the system, program or organization to begin the

process of allowing people to prepare for the transition. Don't wait until the change is just about to be implemented.

Identifying the problem requires information gathering, planning, implementing, and transitioning. You'll need to know what your contingency plans are in case of a critical event takes place due to the problem before the problem can be fully addressed.

Once the resources have been identified, select members for the change management action team. These members must have an appropriate experience base, represent each line of the system or operation and be able to see the process to completion from planning, to implementation and through the transition phases. It is possible to have a separate transition management team but you must ensure there are members of the change management action team who will provide a consistent link throughout the process. Creating a Terms of Reference document will help to define the group's tasks, budget parameters and team outputs. Here are some terms to consider:

Identification of the change management action team

- Size of the team will depend on the scope and scale of the change project.
- Ensure the experience base of the individuals is appropriate for the project.
- Provide change management and transition management training or orientation for the group to ensure understanding of the team's tasks and challenges in guiding the change process.

Duties of the change management team

- Assigning roles and responsibilities (leadership, communication plan, documentation, etc.)
- Facilitating a gap analysis (what processes are already in place to handle the new system and what areas need to be developed)
- Development of the change management plan
- Detailed planning for further change management processes
- Development of the change implementation plan
- Facilitate the progress of the implementation plan
- Develop the transition management plan
- Implement the change safety assurance processes
- Ensure the transition throughout the three phases is closely monitored and managed.

We've mentioned Gap Analysis, but it bears explaining. A gap analysis is a tool to help determine what policies, procedures, guides, manuals, training, and other arrangements which are already in place and might readily receive the change and where there are holes or gaps that may require further development. The gap analysis may also help determine where there are vulnerabilities that arise as consequences of the introduction and interaction between people and the specific features of the change.

Once the Gap Analysis is complete, ensure it is well detailed and incorporated into the documentation process. The items that are identified as missing or deficient will then form the basis for the change management plan which will ensure the implementation will address these items.

The change management process must be clearly communicated in order to ensue continuous support and commitment by leadership, the change management action team and the workforce within the program or system affected. Communicate the reason for the change by actually 'selling the problem'. Do it early and often before you try and share the change itself, the problem, and the change process is clearly understood by those in the planning process, leadership and the workforce that the change will eventually impact, it must be properly communicated.

The change management training is an important part of the communications plan. However, training usually occurs at particular intervals and may not be convenient for necessary information events. The communication plan should:

1. Explain the change management policies, procedures and responsibilities to those involved
2. Describes the channels of communication used to gather and disseminate change management information.
3. Identify triggers that should activate an information flow for both anticipated and unanticipated events.

The communication plan continually provides ongoing information regarding activities and safety performance and encourages continued commitment by the program, system or community the change is affecting. Consider a variety of means when developing the plan; electronic media such as email, twitter, websites, social media accounts, as well as traditional communication through newsletters, bulletins, seminars and training events. Continually be looking for new and useful methods of communication that may benefit the information sharing process.

The information disseminated must be timely, clearly understood and credible. It should be specific to the intended group so they are not overloaded with irrelevant information that may create a lack of interest and eventually a lack of participation. The goal is to keep people engaged, not overburden them.

Information relies on feedback in order for it be communication. Feedback from the program, system or community is necessary to achieve the objectives of the plan as well as having the ability to understand the impacts during the phases of the transition periods. Feedback requires confidence in the system and an assurance that information will be used appropriately. Policies should be specific regarding data confidentiality and the ethical use of information provided by the program, system or field.

Feedback from the field provides valuable information to the change management plan, not only in recognizing the progress of the plan, but in adjusting tactics as necessary to continue toward success. It also is a tool that provides learning events for future change management plans and the continuous improvement process. In order to keep the feedback system healthy, responses to field reports needs to be identified in the communication plan. If people don't receive timely responses with some indication of follow up activity, they may stop participating rendering the communication process ineffective.

Each change that it implemented into a system must be

addressed individually with each unique process that presents itself. Not every change plan will work for every situation; some change processes can be implemented all at once, while others will require implementation in stages. The stage or phased approach is often considered for the larger changes where it can tested, evaluated, adjusted and then expanded to other areas. Either way, ensure the implementation of the change does not outpace the resources or plan. This would likely ensure a complete loss of boundaries and controls during the transition period and a high potential of failure.

Here is a list of questions that will help the organization understand its transition readiness. The important aspect of this assessment process is to get feedback from as wide a set of sources as possible.

EVALUATING THE ORGANIZATIONS READINESS:

1. Is there a sense among the workforce that a change is necessary to address a known problem?
2. Do most people accept that whatever change is taking place represents a valid and effective response to the underlying problem?
3. Does the proposed change polarize the workforce in any way that will make the transition more disruptive?
4. Is the level of trust in the organizations leadership adequate? If it is low, it will be very difficult to bring people along.
5. Will the organization provide people with adequate training for the new situation and roles?
6. Is there a means to capture mistakes and their affects?
7. Does the change fit into a widely understood strategy with a fairly clear vision of the future?
8. Do people understand why they will have to be letting go of existing systems? Is it talked about publicly?
9. Is the cultural memory of the organization open to change or has it been scared by past failures?
10. Has the change been explained to those who are going to be affected by it in as much detail as is currently possible?
11. Are there people within the organization who have experience in change and transition management?

12. Are there people within the organization who have experience in change and transition management?
13. Do the leaders of the change understand that the transitions will take considerably longer to complete than the change?
14. Has the organization set up some way to monitor the progress of the transition?
15. Is the organization prepared to help employees deal with the problems they encounter during the transition or are they pretty much left on their own?

The more negative answers, the more difficult the transition will likely will be. If you develop an effective communication strategy before implementing any of the steps above, you are more likely to have buy-in to the change.

A communication strategy is designed to help you and your organization communicate effectively and meet core organizational objectives. Below we will look at the key elements of a communication strategy.

WRITING YOUR COMMUNICATION STRATEGY

1. **Purpose Statement** – It is useful to say up front why you have developed a communication strategy and what you hope to achieve with it. This does not need to be very detailed, it acts a reference and reminder for those using in their work.

2. **Your Current Situation** – The introductory part of the communications strategy should briefly outline what your organization does, what its main functions are and where it operates. It should also look at your organization's communications strengths – what has been successful and what hasn't worked well in the past.

3. **Organizational objectives and communications objectives** – Any communications strategy should closely reflect your overall organizational plan. In this section you should look at your organization's overall vision and core aims and objectives. You should then suggest how communications can help deliver these goals.

It's important that your communications objectives should be seen to contribute to the achievement of the overall objectives of the organization. In this way they will be recognized not as an add on, but something as fundamental as operational or policy objectives to achieving the organization's overall mission.

4. **Identify Stakeholders** – In this section, you should give a detailed description of your main audiences – both external and internal. You might also refer to potential audience that your organization is keen to connect with. Many organizations will find that they have lots of audiences who they need to interact with. One part of the strategy might look at which audiences will be interested in which parts of your organization or activities. Understanding this may make it easier to prioritize your communications work.

5. **Messages** – Once you have identified your audiences, the next task is to break down your objectives into relevant messages for each of those audiences. Start with the audiences that are the highest priority.

6. **Key Communications Methods** – For each audience identified in your previous section, you should now indicate the most appropriate channels for communicating with them. These might include an e-bulletin, conference, workshop, leaflet, press release, event – or broader methods such as media and your website.

7. **Work Plan** – With your audiences and key communications methods identified, the next step is to draw up a table that indicates the key communications activities, budget and resources allocated to delivering the strategy.

8. **Evaluating Success** – Your communications strategy should conclude with a section on evaluation. What does success look like and how will you know when objectives have been met? Here you should indicate the tools you will use to evaluate various sections of your communications. These could be simple measures such as the

number of responses to e-bulletins, hits to your website or increases in donations following a mail-out. They could be focused on policy changes, for example have the key calls of your campaign been achieved? You could also include measures of media coverage; not only in terms of volume, but also breadth and depth. How often were your key messages mentioned and has there been a shift in public attitude on issues you've been campaigning for?

CHAPTER X

DEVELOP PROCESS-IMPROVING STRATEGIES

WE'VE EXPLORED MANY DIFFERENT facets of business from A – Z. Now, we will bring all of the elements previously discussed together and help you to transition into new ways of thinking and new styles of leadership that may enhance your processes. We'll begin with revisiting effectively diagnosing and continuously improving critical processes within your organization.

First, you must fully understand what a critical process is. It is a business process that must be restored immediately after a disruption to ensure the affected firm's ability to protect its assets, meet its critical needs, and satisfy mandatory regulations and requirements.

How do you do this? One way would be to use the critical questions approach. This a method of assessing behavior in which answers to structured but open ended questions are analyzed against a predetermined criteria.

There are numerous ways to approach critical reasoning questions. We will outline one process in a way that will speak to everyone. We've all taken a test at some point or another. For some test takers, detailed diagramming unlocks the answer. However, for others, this technique proves cumbersome and confusing. Consequently, we cannot emphasize enough the importance of practicing and developing a method for attacking critical reasoning problems that works for you. Below, you will find one possible approach:

Write down A B C D E in your erasable notebook in vertical order. (After A, drop down a line and write B, drop down another line and write C, etc.) As you go through answer choices, you will cross out wrong choices. This saves mental energy and prevents careless mistakes (e.g. you store the answer in your mind, only to recall the wrong answer when you input it into the computer). It is important to write the answer grid down before you read the stimulus or the question stem because writing the letters A, B, C, D, and E weakens your memory of the question stem and stimulus you just read.

At this point, there are two different options. You should experiment with both and discover what works best for you.

Begin by Reading the Question Stem.
1. Since your mental framework for reading the stimulus should be different depending upon the type of the question you are being asked (e.g. a strengthen/weaken versus inference versus identify the conclusion), it is important to read the question stem before reading the stimulus. This allows you to read the argument (stimulus) with the best mental framework.
2. When the appropriate framework for reading the stimulus in mind, read the stimulus. Identify the conclusion (presuming there is one, which is the case most of the time).
3. Quickly re-read the question stem.

Begin by Reading the Stimulus

1. In order to save precious time, begin by reading the stimulus. Reading the question stem first takes additional time since you will likely need to re-read the question stem after reading the stimulus.
2. Read the question stem.
3. Attempt to anticipate the correct answer. This helps prevent your mind from reading the answer choices blind and being persuaded (or duped) by crafty answers designed to trap you.
4. Read the answer choices.
5. Select the correct answer choice.

Using an example from old school days helps you to see this process in real world context. How this applies to business is simple. For every business there is a distinct process involved. Each of our businesses will vary greatly, but the principle is the same, ask critical questions to gain a full three hundred sixty degree view of the problem, whatever that may be. Obviously, if your business doesn't include tangible products made in-house, you wouldn't need to ask questions pertaining to that manufacturing process, but your business may share characteristics as far as customer service issues or human resources.

Enterprises are beginning to understand that consistent customer service is the key to remaining competitive in today's market. A critical step in meeting customer expectations involves clearly defining and prioritizing core business processes.

In today's business environment, organizations know that to be competitive, they need to respond to change – especially as customer expectations increase. Customers are more mobile today, and so expect a certain level of quality of service regardless of where and how they conduct business. Customers also expect organizations to respond with a significant amount of personalization.

It is extremely difficult to meet these challenges in a timely manner if business processes are widely dispersed and inconsistent. Consistent core business processes and data representations is essential to allow decision makers to respond quickly to the changing market.

Defining and maintaining consistent core business processes is a lot easier said than done but critical if an organization is to survive in today's market. Another way to look at core business processes is to think of it as the minimum individual tasks to be accomplished to provide a certain level of consistency in output – without any consideration to hardware, software, or performance.

When a core process is implemented, anything can be added to make the process more efficient, but nothing can be eliminated. When the core business process states that certain tasks must be performed in sequence, then it must be reflected in the implementation. In the same manner, any specified formulas or steps associated with a task must also be reflected within the implementation.

When asked, most organizations will claim that their core business processes are documented. Yet, typically, it is not the core business process that has been documented but the implementation of that process within a particular system. In this scenario, the documentation contains system or application process models reflecting implementation details such as 'enter username.' Most times, documentation of a core business process doesn't reflect whether a user is identified by a username, smart card, biometrics, or some other method of authentication, as long as the organization is satisfied with the accuracy of the documentation. Identifying and authenticating a user is an implementation issue, not a business process.

It's not easy to separate implementation from the core business process. Just take one business process and see how readily you can identify the major tasks involved without letting implementation issues creep into the mix.

And it only gets more difficult when core business processes become more intricate and critical within the enterprise.

Using the right process methodology

The methodology used to identify, derive, or create core business processes will vary with an enterprise's size, industry and culture

But there are several proven methodologies and supporting tools for deriving and improving business processes.

THE FIRST THREE STEPS ARE STRAIGHTFORWARD:

1. Investigate and remove hurdles relating to organizational cultural issues, governance processes, and supporting infrastructure up front.
2. Educate participants on what a core business process is, how it will benefit their respective business area, and the chosen methodology that will be used to derive these processes.
3. Don't try and do all of the critical business processes at once. Suggest a phase approach with a sound transition strategy.

Once you've identified core business processes, it's important to prioritize which ones to tackle first. A new business channel is a good place to start, as business analysis and requirements gathering have likely already been done, which should provide a good jumping off point for identifying core processes. Next, tackle any business process areas featuring disparate results between business units. Then, look at processes for which new enabling technology is being considered. Rounding out the list are those processes supported by different implementation and those supported by more than one location or business.

It's never too late to start.

If enterprises are to remain competitive, they need to reduce the complexities resulting from widely dispensed and often disparate business processes. Establishing consistent core business processes is just one step toward meeting increasing customer expectation in today's market.

BUSINESS PROCESS IMPROVEMENTS

Another approach not yet discussed is the Business Process Improvements (BPI) The demand to improve your business continues to increase as expectations change, new technologies emerge and competition grows. An effective way to establish continual improvement within your organization is to conduct regular BPI's.

Business processes can be informal or formal and touch a variety of company functions: information technology, employee development and training, customer service satisfaction, etc. Regardless of the process you are trying to enhance, the improvement procedure follows a similar path.

1. **Identify the Need for Change:** The first step in the BPI process is to identify the need for change. A useful way to discover improvement opportunities is by conducting a process audit. The audit will identify current issues or potential risks for your company. From the audit report you will be able to prioritize your areas for areas for business improvement. At this stage, you should also review how each process impacts your organization, resources and stakeholders (employees, customers, students, partners, supplies, etc.).

2. **Analyze Current Process:** Once you have decided which process you are going to improve you need to analyze the current procedure. This way you can fully understand the process from A – Z and set realistic improvement objectives. Regardless of the tool you choose for analysis (process mapping, operational surveys, cause/effect analysis, etc.) you should consider the following questions:

    *   What in the process is broken?
    *   Which steps in the process create roadblocks?
    *   Which step requires the most time to complete?
    *   Which step causes the most delays?
    *   Are there any steps that cause costs/resources to go up?
    *   Are there any steps that cause quality to go down?

3. **Obtain Commitment and Support:** The third step in the process is to solicit senior management commitment. This is possibly the single most important element in the process as the success of the project hinges

on managerial support. At this stage you need to clearly present the necessity for change and how it impacts the organization. It is crucial that management understands the need for change to ensure they will support recommendations. As process improvement can be time and resource intensive upper management support is a must.

4. **Create Improvement Strategy:** With the process analysis phase completed you need to develop your strategy. It is recommended that you include what steps in the process are broken, why and how they should be improved and any financial and resource implications. Answering how the process can be improved is a springboard to create your improvement objectives. It is recommended that you set realistic and measurable objectives that align with your overall strategic goals.

Five Steps to a Workable Business Process Management Strategy

Building a business process management strategy needn't be overly complex. Here's how to get started in five steps that can scale with your business.

If you ever thought about a business process management system was too complex and too time consuming to prove successful in your business, think again. Even a small company with little resources can develop a business process management strategy that will help the business streamline processes and become more efficient, just as their larger competitor are.

Due to their size and nature, organizations may actually be better positioned for process management success than larger enterprises. The smaller the organization, the more favorable the environment for achieving big changes.

For smaller businesses the political issues are somewhat smaller and the opportunity to make great strides forward is greater. Awareness and documentation doesn't need to be bone crunching to deliver some strong return on investment and fast results.

And sometimes, you may not have to go as far as you think to achieve a successful process management plan. Smaller firms are generally more flexible and this may work to their advantage when it comes to process improvement efforts.

Here are some steps to begin and eventually build a business process management strategy:

Identify a business team that has historically worked well together.

Have them brainstorm a cross functional process that needs improvement. That doesn't mean a massive project; an initial effort should aim to improve one or two processes at most.

Conservatively estimate the potential savings of the improvement.

When attempting to gain funding, ensure that the team provides management with a list of follow on projects that can also use the proposed tools.

Execute the process improvement project with the best project manager you can find to lead the initial effort. This is important because getting staff members on board is often a more difficult task than choosing a BPM tool because both business and other teams have to be comfortable and willing to follow the new policies and processes.

During the project, watch for bottlenecks.

Document lessons learned and use this information to guide additional efforts. Then, project by project, build a culture of continued process improvement and increased business efficiency that fits your organization's BPM maturity level.

HOW TO ENSURE THAT THE CONCEPTS YOU LEARNED CAN BE IMPLEMENTED

THERE ARE A NUMBER OF REASONS why ideas fail to become concepts or innovations. Sometimes it is because the idea, which seems brilliant in concept, is flawed in application. More often, the problem is that organizations invest in creative ideation initiatives (often called 'innovation initiatives'), such as brainstorming events, idea management, ideas campaigns and the like, but fail to invest in implementing the most creative ideas that come from those initiatives.

Indeed, you have probably experienced this typical scenario:

a company invests in generating ideas via brainstorming events that involve a lot of highly paid managers and researchers. A number of promising creative ideas generated. Sometimes business plans are developed. Sometimes prototypes are built. Sometimes not. But, at some point between the identification of a promising idea and beginning to implement that idea, the idea is killed.

There are many reasons why ideas are killed, however, almost all of them have to do with risk. Implementing a new idea is perceived as risky and people in the company do not wish to undertake that risk. So, the idea is killed. Needless to say, investing in a creative idea generation initiative in order to generate creative or innovative ideas you will never implement is an expensive method of accomplishing absolutely nothing.

Unwillingness to implement innovative ideas is not only a weakness with companies, individuals have the same problem. Imagine a young person applying for a job at a high profile tech company or apparel company and having the idea to write her CV (resume in US English) on a piece of clothing (in the case of an apparel company) and sending it to his or her perspective employer. Such a creative or innovative approach to applying for a job would almost certainly stand out and grab the attention of the hiring person. It could very well result in an interview – particularly if the company values innovation as most apparel and tech companies do. Or it could result in the CV (resume) imprinted clothing being promptly rubbished as ridiculous.

Such a waste of creative time, energy and money does no one any good and makes the world a more boring place than it should be.

In order to help individuals and organizations more rationally plan the implementation of innovative ideas, we can look at why ideas are not implemented (at the organizational level and individual level) and have drawn up an (Innovative) Creative Idea Implementation Plan.

THE IDEA
Before you implement your idea, you need to describe it in detail.

Separately, you should describe what makes the idea special, that is: what is he unique selling point? Once you have done this, ask yourself how you might push the unique selling point (i.e. buy-in) even further in order to make your idea even more special.

BENEFITS AND RISKS

The next step is to do a simple risk versus benefits analysis. That may sound complex, but might simply be a matter of drawing up a table with a column labeled benefits and one called risks. Then simply lists the benefits and risks in their appropriate columns. If the risks are greater than the benefits, you need to rethink your idea and focus on greater benefits. Review your unique sales price in particular.

STUMBLING BLOCKS

A stumbling block is something that can stop, damage or destroy your implementation before it is complete. Early stumbling blocks, such as getting approval from a notoriously conservative committee, lack of budget or risk adverse managers can kill an innovative idea at an early stage of its implementation. To prevent this from happening, you should list all of the possible stumbling blocks that exist between now and the successful implementation of your idea. Then look at each stumbling block and indicate how you will deal with it. Being prepared for stumbling blocks not only makes it easier to get past them, but also impresses the people who are responsible for the stumbling blocks. (And most stumbling blocks are caused by people.)

PEOPLE

Speaking of people, make a list of people – as well as organizations and groups – who should be involved in your implementation. These may be colleagues who will buy into your idea, making it easier to sell to top management or they may be designers who will build a prototype to demonstrate your idea or an engineer who is building a new component or any number of professionals who are bringing an idea to fruition. A complex business idea often requires the involvement of numerous people.

AUTHORIZATIONS

Implementing the idea may include the necessity of gaining authorizations from one or more bodies. Authorizations may include approval from people in your company, licenses from government offices and certificates from professional organizations or bodies. If an idea is in a new area, it is best to research relevant government regulations – you may be in for a surprise. Some of what they require will go from the common sense side of life to absolutely ludicrous.

MONEY

Calculate the costs of implementing your idea and what is the likely income. For most business ideas, you will probably want to prepare a cash flow table to calculate the costs and income over time. If you can demonstrate a cash flow with minimal outlay and a large reward potential, you will find it significantly easier to convince to buy into your idea.

MILESTONES

With all but the simplest ideas, you should draw up a list of milestones that must be achieved along the way towards implementing your idea. For example, a new product idea might require a business case, a prototype, market research, product testing, etc. In addition, milestones can be good points for determining whether or not to continue with an idea; or for considering modifications to the idea.

ESCAPE PLAN

Very often, when considering implementing an innovative idea, committees will water down the idea and make it less risky. Unfortunately, removing risk from an idea is the same as removing creativity. An innovative idea with its risk removed is often a mediocre idea. A better approach is to go ahead with a risky, creative idea, but to have an escape plan. For example: if the idea does not meet certain milestones within a determined time frame, you agree to stop it. And so on. Predetermining an escape plan mitigates risk and ensures you and your company you will not continue to throw money at an idea that eventually proves unlikely to meet its potential.

COMMUNICATION PLAN

A communication plan clarifies who should learn about the implementation, when they should learn about it and how. A communication plan may also indicate who should not know about the idea implementation, particularly at the early stages. For instance, if you are working on a breakthrough idea, you may want to keep it secret as long as possible to prevent your competitors from learning what you are doing. On the other hand, you might want to communicate about your highly innovative idea immediately in order to be recognized as the first moving innovator behind the new idea.

Even if you are implementing a personal idea, communicating it can help give you the confidence to see it through to completion. Moreover, discussing the idea with friends, family and colleagues may provide valuable input about how to make the idea more innovative.

ACTION PLAN

The last step of the implementation plan is the step by step action plan. This will describe every step you take, how long each step will take and what should be achieved. It will incorporate much of the information above. Indeed, by compiling the information above first, you can better develop a cast iron action plan that increases the likeliness that your idea will be implemented effectively. And that is what turns an innovative idea into an innovation.

Having ideas is easy. Having creative or innovative visions is harder. Implementing them is most challenging of all, but it doesn't have to be impossible.

If you really want to turn your idea into reality, you need to make a decision to implement it. That may seem like a small thing, but for many people it is a huge step. Innovative concepts are wonderful, but can be intimidating when it comes time to implement them. However, if you do not make a decision, you will not implement your vision.

ACTION PLANNING

Once you have made the decision to move forward and do something about your concept, you need to start thinking of your creative vision as a goal rather than a vision. This may mean reformulating the way you think about your vision. That' okay. Innovation should be flexible.

Once you have your goal in mind, you need to draw up an action plan. If the goal is simple to implement, your action plan can also be simple:

ACTION PLAN
1. Do it.

However this is seldom the case! Assuming your goal is more complex, you need to deconstruct it into much smaller steps, or sub-goals, each of which is as simple (or nearly as simple) as the one above, and which together plot a path from where you are now to the achievement of your goal.

The best way to do this is to commandeer a big table. Take a couple of sheets of paper. One, write 'you are here' in a circle – like you see on those maps on signboards on city streets and nature trails. On another sheet of paper, write down your goal in a few words. Put one sheet at either end of the table.

Now, get a stack of small sheets of paper: index cards, notepad sheets or – if you want to be environmentally friendly – used printer paper cut into quarters. Look at 'you are here' and look at your goal and think about what you need to do to get from one to the other. Write down each envisioned action on one of the small papers and put it in the middle of the table. Do not worry about orientation or placement now. Do not worry about overlapping actions or possibly unnecessary actions. Just toss each sheet into the middle of the table.

STRUCTURE

Once you have exhausted your mind of necessary steps, start organizing all the pieces of paper. Make a trail of steps from 'you are here' to your goal. Try to lay out the steps in a structured way. For example, papers with overlapping actions can overlap physically as well. I there seems to be a distance between to sequential actions, put a distance between the papers.

When you are finished, look at your path and each action. Are there redundant actions? If so, remove them. Are there gaps in the path? If so, look at the actions on either side of the gap, think about what action needs to be taken in order to bridge the gap. Write the action down and add it to the path.

Once you have done this, envision performing each action. How do you feel about it? Is it an easy action to implement? If so, that's great. If it is complicated or overwhelming, you probably need to deconstruct that action into smaller actions.

If an action feels intimidating, ask yourself why? Perhaps it obliges you to make a presentation to a large group of people which frightens you. Perhaps it asks you to ask a favor of someone you do not like. Perhaps it asks you to do something ethically questionable. If so, rethink the action. Can you really do it? If not, find an alternative method of performing this action. Because if you leave this action in the sequence of steps, from "you are here" to your goal, and you are unable to perform the action, you will endanger the implementation of your vision. Better to deal with difficult steps now, when you are feeling optimistic (you are feeling optimistic, aren't you?) rather than leave them for later.

On the other hand, if an action merely puts you outside of your comfort zone, then keep it in the sequence, but think about whether additional action is necessary. For instance, if you have to give a public presentation, but that makes you uncomfortable, then you might add an additional step, such as signing up for a public speaking training course or joining toastmasters (a club for practicing public speaking).

FIND SOMETHING FUN IN EACH ACTION

Once you have finalized the actions, go through them again, one by one. For each action, find something fun or positive about performing the action. Sometimes this will be easy. Sometimes it will not. But, if you can find something to look forward to in each action, it will increase the likelihood that you do the action and that, in turn, increases the likelihood that your creative vision is realized.

MILESTONES

If the goal is elaborate, will require a significant investment or will have bad consequences if it fails, you should include milestones in your action plan. A milestone is some kind of reference point against which you can measure progress.

As you come to each milestone, stop, review progress and determine whether or not you have met the terms of the milestone. If not, you must review the project, determine what went wrong and determine whether you can fix the situation or whether you should kill the implementation and work on a new, creative project.

This is important. Once you get going on a creative project, it is easy to become emotionally attached to it. That can make you reluctant to kill the project even if it is failing. However, some creative goals do fail. They are by nature original, untried and untested. You are trying and testing the goal. Maybe it will not work. If not, don't worry and, more importantly, do not waste additional resources. Kill the project and work on something else.

Of course this does not mean that whenever things go wrong, you should kill the project! Sometimes problems can be fixed. Sometimes you need to adjust your expectations. If this is the case, make the necessary changes in your action plan and get back to work!

COLLABORATIVE ACTION PLANNING

If you are collaborating on this creative goal, you need to assign responsibilities for each step in the sequence. If you do not, everyone in the group will expect someone else to take action and nothing will happen!

First, decide who is in charge of the overall goal. Very likely it will be you. So, I am going to assume it is you!

Put your name on the sheet of paper with the goal written on it and acknowledge to the group that you will oversee and coordinate the implementation of the goal.

Then go to the first step and decide who is responsible for the step. Ask her if she has any concerns about her ability to perform the step. If so, address those concerns as described above. If not, or once the concerns are satisfactorily addressed, ask her "will you take responsibility for [step 1]?" Ensure she replies in the positive. Then ask her to write her name on the step.

It may seem a bit silly asking someone if she will perform a step and asking her to sign the step. But this ensures each member of the group acknowledges his or her responsibility towards the project and the group which, in turn, increases the likelihood that she performs her part in the project's implementation.

This is important. If one person fails to perform her step, it undermines the implementation of the goal and could kill the project! This happens far more often than it should!

REVIEW DEVELOPMENT

In addition to measuring progress against milestones, review overall progress on a regular basis and be prepared to modify steps as necessary. As noted, your goal is untested. As a result, some steps are almost certain not to go exactly as expected. A step may not be achievable. Something may go wrong. A particular step may prove impossible

Mind you, the unexpected is not always negative. You may find that a particular step works out better than expected. Perhaps it costs far less than expected to implement or brings even better results than anticipated.

In addition, you make discoveries as you progress towards implementing the goal. You may have ideas about how to make the goal better, how to get there faster or how to get even better results. Others may want to help you in implementing your goal. Do not refuse these opportunities simply because you have a plan. Change the plan accordingly. Creativity requires flexibility.

When things do not work out as expected, whether in a positive or a negative way, you will probably need to rethink and very likely modify subsequent steps. Do not be afraid to do this. In extreme cases, you may even need to go back to the table and the pieces of paper in order to rethink the action plan. There's nothing wrong with that. Do it.

You may even need to kill the project. As noted above, if this is necessary, do it.

VISUALIZING YOUR GOAL
If you have read up on personal development, you will recognize aspects of the inner-mind approach to implementing a vision. That's not surprising. Personal development is about defining and achieving goals – and implementing a vision is pretty much the same thing, but with a lot more creativity added.

However, many self-help gurus suggest that you always keep the goal in mind. They insist that you visualize your goal regularly. Think about how wonderful you will feel once you have achieved it. Think about the benefits. They claim that this will motivate you towards achieving your goal.

They are wrong.

LAW OF DISTRACTION
Some gurus even cite *the Law of Attraction*, which roughly says that if you think about achieving your goal hard enough, you will attract

success and your goal will come true. Somehow, the law implies, the Universe will make this happen. This, of course, is ridiculous. The Universe does not really care about your goals or what you do.

Moreover, research has shown that if you fantasize about achieving your goal, your mind will start to anticipate the pleasure and satisfaction of success. Indeed, your mind will feel so good about the fantasy, it will lose interest in the implementation. In experiments, people who fantasize about achieving their goals are less energized than those who do not. Worse, they are less likely to achieve their goals than those who do not fantasize.

Moreover, having only positive thoughts about a fantasized future makes you less likely to see the potential pitfalls and obstacles you will likely face on the road to achieving your goal, which will leave you unprepared to follow the path from where you are to achieving your goal.

GREAT EXPECTATIONS

On the other hand, expectation that you will achieve your goal increases the likelihood that you will succeed. Why is this? It is because expectation comes from experience. If you have had similar experiences with positive outcomes, you know what is required and can be more confident about achieving your goal. Thanks to experience, you are also more likely to be aware of – and better prepared for – the pitfalls, obstacles and challenges you will face along the way.

ABOUT THE AUTHOR

Ravinder Tulsiani, is a renowned Leadership Expert, Author and Speaker. He has appeared in several major media outlets including Bloomberg, CNN and Wall Street Journal and is the author of numerous quality, business and self-help resources.

With over 13 years of industry experience, Ravinder's reputation for excellence reflects his expertise as a strategic planner, who creates cultural transformation in business, focusing on educating and motivating the workforce to achieve core business objectives.

Ravinder is not only a Certified Training & Development Professional (CTDP) with a Masters Certificate in Adult Training & Development and Human Resources Management Diploma, but has a Canadian Investment Manager (CIM) accreditation and is a Fellow of the Canadian Securities Institute (FCSI).

Ravinder has compiled his wealth of industry experience and his business acumen to comprise *Your Leadership Edge – Mastering Management Skills For Today's Workforce* so that industry professionals can unlock their leadership potential using his proven step-by-step program.

PRACTICAL LEADERSHIP GUIDE
FOR THE WORKPLACE

Printed in Great Britain
by Amazon.co.uk, Ltd.,
Marston Gate.